Flee!

The Coming Conflict between Freedom and Religion

Richard J. Rosica, Jr.

World rights reserved. This book or any portion thereof may not be copied or reproduced in any form or manner whatever, except as provided by law, without the written permission of the publisher, except by a reviewer who may quote brief passages in a review.

This book was written to provide truthful information in regard to the subject matter covered. The author assumes full responsibility for the accuracy of all facts and quotations as cited in this book. The opinions expressed in this book are the author's personal views and interpretation of the Bible, Spirit of Prophecy, and/or contemporary authors and do not necessarily reflect those of TEACH Services, Inc.

This book is sold with the understanding that the publisher is not engaged in giving spiritual, legal, medical, or other professional advice. If authoritative advice is needed, the reader should seek the counsel of a competent professional.

Copyright © 2013 TEACH Services, Inc.
ISBN-13: 978-1-4796-0050-2 (Paperback)
ISBN-13:1-4796-0051-9 (ePub)
ISBN-13: 1-4796-0052-6 (Kindle / Mobi)
Library of Congress Control Number: 2013935119

All scripture quotations are taken from the King James Version Bible.

Published by

www.TEACHServices.com • (800) 367-1844

Table of Contents

Preface		v
Chapter 1	Of Rhetoric and Rationales	10
Chapter 2	"My People"	14
Chapter 3	Crucial Realities and Common Sense	20
Chapter 4	Been There, Done That—How History Reveals Prophecy	29
Chapter 5	Religious Persecution—A Historical Legacy	36
Chapter 6	He Shall Think to Change the Times...	42
Chapter 7	A Delegation of Power—How Satan Uses Men	49
Chapter 8	Back in Business—The Healing of the Beast	55
Chapter 9	The False Prophet—Not Who You Might Expect	58
Chapter 10	Antichrist	64
Chapter 11	The Enduring Fable—Ye Shall Not Surely Die	71
Chapter 12	Spiritualism—Miracle or Mass Deception?	78
Chapter 13	The Times We Are In	84
Chapter 14	The Sabbath—It's About Worship	93
Chapter 15	Ritual and Ruin	99

Chapter 16 Ecumenism—The Unity Façade 104

Chapter 17 Armageddon—It Happened in the Valley 113

Chapter 18 Every Eye Will See Him—The Second Coming 119

Preface

The question has been asked—if one were locked in a dream, how would they know the difference between the dream world and the real? We have all been there, fantasizing that we can fly or that we are falling, feeling as though someone is pursuing us or that we are in pursuit of something. Many of us have imagined ourselves rich, poor, popular and even naked in public. Who among us has not had such an experience? Upon awakening from those kinds of images there are three likely reactions: amusement because it was interesting, relief because it was not real, or disappointment because we wanted it to be. Though one may wish to continue dreaming, our only choice is to file the experience away in our memory where it gradually fades away.

There is another type of dream, one that is not limited to the realm of unconsciousness, one that people are equally unaware of until someone or something finally wakes them up. Once a person discovers that they cannot actually soar above a crowd like a blimp, teleport from country to country or did not really have that winning lottery ticket, there is nothing a person can do to change that reality. When one realizes they have been living in a fantasy, their reaction, whether it is joy, relief, disappointment or even anger, must invoke a response. Waking to find one's house burning requires definitive action, but if one is woken only to find out their house needs a new paint job, there will obviously be a less urgent response. It seems that whether we are trying to convince someone that their property is on the verge of becoming a vacant lot or that their unsightly exterior merely brings down real estate values on the block, the problem is less about the solution than waking people to the truth. A bucket of water means nothing to a person who will not see the flames.

Today, the spiritual lives of millions are based on a complex and enticing façade of manufactured religion and baseless theology. These amalgamations of human philosophy, misinterpretations of scripture, and psychological appeasements have many people trapped in belief systems that pose grave danger when they are not shown the way of escape. The enemy has successfully planted seeds of error, which have grown to become a normal part of many Christian experiences. With the conscious option to remain in one's delusion, the question then becomes about how they will react when they are awakened, if they indeed can be. Will they open their heart to the solution or will they choose to go back to sleep?

In the preface of his wonderfully insightful book *Mere Christianity*, C. S. Lewis describes the gradual spoilage of the word, "Christian." In its original context, Lewis observes that a Christian is expressly referred to a person who has "accepted the teachings of the gospel." Over time, the word has become refined and spiritualized to refer simply to an overall religious character, placing little or no emphasis on adherence to a specific set of beliefs. Unfortunately, as Lewis also points out, this shift in the true definition of "Christian" renders the word useless because no one has the ability or the right to judge the heart of another person and no one should understand that better than a Christian.

Lewis compares this refinement to the watered-down definition of a "gentleman." To paraphrase, a gentleman was once described as a man who had obtained a distinct level of real estate and social status regardless of reputation. Now, the word applies to a man with a favorable personality and temperament. Unfortunately, the use of gentleman in this manner conveys no specific or quantifiable information—only subjective, third-party impressions of the man in question. Using this analogy, Lewis submits that the only way we can effectively use the word "Christian" is to "stick to the original, obvious meaning." He remarks that the issue is not "theological or moral." Accordingly, we should agree that a lousy plumber is still a plumber, an attorney who embraces frivolous lawsuits is still an attorney, and an honest politician is still a politician. Lastly, as Lewis says, a person who does not live up to the gospel they profess might have others deem them a "bad Christian" rather than saying they are not a Christian at all.

Although I agree with Mr. Lewis' perceptions and analogy, it puts my writing in an awkward position because it runs the risk of creating a false impression. I am not suggesting that we can or should classify anyone who holds on to various errors as bad Christians or even go so far as to deny them the title altogether. On the contrary, there are people in many churches who have accepted the gospel as they understand it and live according to that knowledge. They demonstrate the love of Christ, and they glorify God in their daily lives as well as through their charitable endeavors. I will refrain from saying that someone who professes a major mistake in doctrine is a non-Christian despite the fact that they claim Jesus as their Lord and Savior, and I do so because I believe we should not judge the heart—I have no way of knowing why someone chooses to believe erroneously. However, what we will learn in the coming chapters is that there are beliefs that show that one might not understand the teachings of the gospel. I will not assume that anyone has taught them correctly or that they have ever rejected the truth. I will only recognize that many hold beliefs that the Bible does not sanction and these concepts harbor profound danger.

This is where the emphasis of this book diverges from Mr. Lewis'. The great writer focused on explaining the core values of Christianity allegedly common to all churches. Lewis assiduously avoided "disputed points" of theology, which he felt unqualified to discuss. He believed his approach was a better strategy for winning new souls to Christ than entertaining those debates. I agree with that assertion. Most Bible study techniques reflect the importance of getting new believers to know and love Christ and what He did for them before that can digest the meatier subjects.

However, I would like to point out that the Bible says nothing about leaving discussions of doctrine to experts. Jesus chose ordinary people for the Great Commission. It is to the glory of God that my theological background is no higher than theirs, and I am profoundly humbled that the Lord has placed me here for this purpose.

My message is not a specific attempt to bring new believers into the fold. However, if someone in the midst of a Bible study or is simply searching for answers is able to find something here to inspire them to give their life to Jesus, all the glory goes to God. The initial purpose of this book will be to discuss doctrine so that those who have already accepted the gospel are not thrown off course. We are addressing those who hold fast to the notion that there is only one God and that Jesus Christ is His only begotten Son. Though these are God's people, many of them are unaware of the danger they face.

Some contested points of theology are simply disputes over trivia. But if we consider every doctrinal disparity with that same mindset, many who claim the promises of the gospel could be disappointed on the last day. Thus, while a discussion of doctrine is not the preferred way to lead people to Jesus, understanding why certain doctrines are dangerous is essential to preventing them from being led astray. If it were not so, the devil would not try so hard to create concepts within the church that steer people to the wrong path. If it were not so, we could ignore texts such as Isaiah 29:24; Matthew 15:9; 2 Timothy 2:3, 4; and 2 Thessalonians 2:10–12. "They also that erred in spirit shall come to understanding, and they that murmured shall learn doctrine (Isa. 29:24).

"But in vain they do worship me, teaching for doctrines the commandments of men" (Matt. 15:9).

"For the time will come when they will not endure sound doctrine; but after their own lusts shall they heap to themselves teachers, having itching ears; And they shall turn away their ears from the truth, and shall be turned unto fables" (2 Tim. 4:3, 4).

"And with all deceivableness of unrighteousness in them that perish; because they received not the love of the truth, that they might be saved. And for this cause God shall send them strong delusion, that they should believe a lie: That they all might be damned who believed not the truth, but had pleasure in unrighteousness" (2 Thess. 2:10–12).

We cannot discuss every doctrinal discrepancy or every fable that might exist in one denomination or another. There are not enough trees to produce the paper. Moreover, writers who tackle delicate subjects of any type are fully aware that their assertions may appear second-hand and outside of their proper context. Remaining sensitive to the modern understanding of "Christian," which C. S. Lewis rightly laments, it will suffice to say that some doctrines are not in harmony with the teachings of Christ. When presented with these facts, the reader must then decide in which pasture they prefer to stand. I hope to help them realize that, in the end, sitting on the fence about doctrine is not a choice they can afford to make.

Contemporary Christianity harbors numerous versions of the truth and an amazing array of prophetic interpretations. Whether intentional or not, error and false teaching result in a form of ignorance even more deadly than unbelief. They result in deception and the defining trait of anyone so encumbered is that they are completely oblivious. The only safeguard, the only sure way to know whether one is walking in harmony with truth, is the Bible.

"Happy is the man that findeth wisdom, and the man that getteth understanding" (Prov. 3:13).

It is difficult to imagine how a person might find fault with a Bible verse like this one. In almost any context the concept is thoughtful and truthful. Who does not want to gain wisdom? Yet, the Bible invariably refers to "understanding" in a spiritual sense, a knowledge of sanctification and holiness, which is not the wisdom most people cherish. Thus, those who do not strive for that kind of knowledge automatically discount almost anything the Bible says. The amazing irony is that many deny the Bible on the basis that men wrote it. Such thinking is the sad legacy of oppressive religion and corrupt theologies intended to control the masses, but the irony of criticizing the Bible does not come from its misuse; it comes by the subtle admission that men are fallible. Any denial of that fact is simply absurd. For doubters, this automatically places scripture in the same category. However, if one actually takes the time to study its testimony, they would conclude that human beings could not have conceived it. It is by studying the Word of God that leads one to acknowledge its true origin:

"All scripture is given by inspiration of God, and is profitable for doctrine, for reproof, for correction, for instruction in righteousness" (2 Tim. 3:16).

We will concede that men put pen to papyrus, wooden tablets, or anything else they may have used to record the scriptures. We will acknowledge that the language, vocabulary and prose also bore the impress of each man, but throughout the Bible, these same men confess to their mere instrumentality in the hand of God. Though they wrote in different styles, every thought they expressed was a revelation from God.

In spite of this amazing work of inspiration, the trend today is to avoid doctrinal discussions for the sake of unity among believers of all denominations and to present an image of love and tolerance to the world. Many submit that the similarities between faiths outweigh the differences to the extent that we should ignore the latter. The concept may seem noble, but it is not informed. As we shall discover, the true motives for ignoring doctrine have deeper and more troubling roots. It should come as no surprise that the enemy wants no one to understand the gospel, but what will come as a surprise are the tactics he uses to prevent people from becoming knowledgeable in the Word of God.

Nonetheless, for the sake of truth, some people should not talk about religious doctrine any more than they should politics. The problems that occur when one speaks of these things are not caused by religion but by human nature. No one likes hearing that they might be in error especially when someone who has a correct understanding of doctrine falls into the temptation to prove themselves right at the expense of decorum and civility. Sports fanatics are such because they gain a sense of satisfaction and even euphoria from victory. Nevertheless, witnessing for Christ has no room for a competitive spirit. Those who gain pleasure from the defeat of their opponents do not emulate the attitude of Jesus. Evangelism and witnessing are not spectator sports.

Victory and self-satisfaction are not my motives for writing, and I did not embark on this effort with any preconceived notions for success. The Lord calls us to be diligent and forthright in sharing the gospel, but in compelling people to believe it, we must leave the heavy lifting to the Holy Spirit.

Nevertheless, my appeal to Christians of good conscience will ruffle many feathers. Jesus could not open every heart to the gospel. By what right (or arrogance) could I presume to do better and still remain faithful to the truth? This is not an exercise in tough love. My goal is not correction, but it is one where I aspire to convey knowledge in a manner that anyone can understand. My heartfelt desire is that people who read this book will not consider any remarks, which may be detrimental to concepts they hold dear, as an assault on their faith or an attempt to win an argument. I am only here to replant seeds of truth. Thus, with no axe to grind and with nothing to gain except the joy of knowing that I have done what God asked, we shall labor (the Holy Spirit and I) to explain this warning to God's people. Although it is not new, the information conveyed here is still of the gravest importance—important because God wants all his people to know how to escape deception, and it is a grave situation because time is running out. This is God's final appeal to loved ones trapped in spiritual Babylon. Flee!

Chapter 1
Of Rhetoric and Rationales

O the depth of the riches both of the wisdom and knowledge of God! how unsearchable are his judgments, and his ways past finding out!
Romans 11:33

If you ask an atheist to give their reasons for unbelief, they generally base them on what they cannot understand about God: why does God allow evil to exist? Why can't we see him? Why do bad things to happen to "good" people? Why do we have mosquitoes? Unfortunately, the amount of time we could spend conceiving these kinds of questions and then groping for answers is endless. It is not within the capabilities of this writer or any other to explain the rationale behind every nuance of divine thinking.

Of course, this is the Achilles heel of such a belief system because the premise of an atheist's question insinuates that God must operate within the confines of their particular form of wisdom. But I submit who are we to tell God how He must operate? Because the Creator of the universe is not bound to a human standard, such a basis for unbelief becomes irrelevant. If we could understand every mystery of God's power, if His will, intellect and foresight for the life of each person did not confound the greatest minds on earth, He would not be God.

"For my thoughts are not your thoughts, neither are your ways my ways, saith the LORD. For as the heavens are higher than the earth, so are my ways higher than your ways, and my thoughts than your thoughts" (Isa. 55:8, 9).

However, we can provide some logic behind an answer to the most provocative questions: why does God allow evil to exist and why do bad things happen to "good" people? Satan is behind the wickedness and evil in the world just as he was in the time of Job. What Satan does not perpetrate directly, he encourages through the lower nature of man. Clearly, this begs the next question … why then does God allow the devil to get away with it?

The effects of sin are beyond comprehension, but without the freedom to choose one's course and either witness or experience the painful effects of sin first hand, one can never understand how much it grieves the heart of God. Despite the discomfort for everyone involved, the Lord must allow evil to run its course for man to understand its nature. Some will undoubtedly demand to know why God would allow it to take so long. There are explanations, but again, there will be no end to the questions for someone who is not truly seeking answers.

It is not that the Lord wanted man to sin. Adam and Eve were unacquainted with evil until they chose to disobey. The tree God placed before them would test their faith, but it was the devil who urged Eve to yield to temptation. After that event, sin would have a progressively negative impact on the world. At the cross and at the end of days, it is the manner in which God has and will deliver man from evil that demonstrates His unimaginable love, unlimited mercy, and unerring judgment.

Whether that profoundly abbreviated explanation proves acceptable to the hearer or even sparks interest in the rest of this book is an open question. It is a sad but sure fact that no matter how sincerely or passionately we try to answer, no matter how persuasive or succinct our logic might be, if someone does not want to believe the truth … they will not.

There is no evidence that God does not exist—only theories that no one will ever prove. There is no proof that Jesus was not the Messiah—only a desire to believe he was not. Science cannot refute the Bible, and the only reason people deny the Word of God is because they choose to. Much to the dismay of unbelievers, God would have it no other way.

The Christian faith on the other hand comes with a plenty of evidence. The wonders of nature, historical events, miracles of healing, and eyewitness accounts of spiritual transformation all testify to the power and presence of an everlasting God. Unfortunately, the world limits its definition of miracles to feats of the grandiose, which they can see or touch. They overlook the Lord's hand in the small things that science cannot explain—the germination of a seed, how butterflies migrate more than 2000 thousand miles or why roses have such a pleasant aroma. These do not appeal to the unbeliever's concept of proof that God exists or that these gifts to mankind are wonderful expressions of love. Instead of embracing the unexplained as a revelation of divine intellect and a blessing we should enjoy and marvel upon, the world measures, catalogues, exploits, and destroys all in the name of "wisdom."

The freedom to reject such testimony does not render the evidence invalid or make the choice of unbelief a prudent one. Strangely though, many people who consider themselves Christian will believe almost anything if it sounds pleasant or biblical enough. I do not mean to offend with such a statement although it undoubtedly will. It is also certain that my readers will demand to know which of their beliefs I refer to. However, much more important than a list of false doctrines are the motives a person has for believing them. This is where the true problem lies.

As I stated in the preface, it is not for me or anyone else to tell someone why they believe something. We cannot discern the motives or intents of the heart, but we can lay out the possibilities and allow people to judge themselves. It may be simple ignorance; perhaps they have never heard the truth. But what if they have? Once presented with the facts, it is for the individual to decide what their destiny will be.

For those who know the truth, the folly of unbelief is both obvious and perplexing. Why people choose to reject the gospel will forever remain a mystery. Militant atheism has no solid foundation, only a preference for the presumptions of science and the philosophy of humanism, neither of which harbors proof of anything. Regarding Christianity as a form of superstition is also not evidence; it is an uninformed opinion. Even when presented with miracles or amazing conversion stories, many do not want to believe that God had a hand in them. So, to placate their fears of divine accountability or fuel their humanistic pride, they gravitate toward any rationale or theory that rejects Him.

This rejection causes much more concern when it comes from those who claim to know the truth. It is troubling because these are denials implicit in doctrines that steer people off the path of sanctification and ultimately away from their very hope of redemption. This is the devil's greatest feat of treachery—lead those to their doom while they sing the praises of God along the way! How is this even possible? Can one claim to know Jesus and still be lost? The Bible gives us an unequivocal answer.

"Not every one that saith unto me, Lord, Lord, shall enter into the kingdom of heaven; but he that doeth the will of my Father which is in heaven. Many will say to me in that day, Lord, Lord, have we not prophesied in thy name? and in thy name have cast out devils? and in thy name done many wonderful works? And then will I profess unto them, I never knew you: depart from me, ye that work iniquity" (Matt. 7:21–23).

Jesus here speaks to those who call themselves disciples falsely. The cry of 'Lord, Lord' will never come from the lips of an unbeliever. It is not enough to believe. Even the devil manages that much (see James 2:19). How can one appear to perform so many works on behalf of Christ and in the end not have His blessing? It comes down to the heart. Jesus tells those who point to their works as justification that they have not done the one thing He truly expects; they have failed to repent of their sins. Despite the biblical evidence otherwise, a mere profession of faith is all that many churches say we need. But if we do not act upon that belief in cooperation with the Holy Spirit to change our hearts, what does that profession mean?

"This people draweth nigh unto me with their mouth, and honoureth me with their lips; but their heart is far from me" (Matt. 15:8).

A pretense of faith is worse than unbelief. There is nothing God detests more than a phony follower. Before they instigated the death of Jesus, the sin that the Pharisees and chief priests in Israel were most guilty of was pride in a superficial, hypocritical religion. It is a condition that much of Christianity has. The words above came straight from the mouth of Christ. Without question, He expunges the notion that everyone who calls Him Lord has built their house on a solid foundation. In short, the Lord himself affirms, you can call yourself a believer and still be lost!

Teachings, which occasionally contradict many fundamentals of the gospel, are prevalent in Christianity. There is only one path to salvation. It is narrow, hard to find, and impossible to navigate, that is, without the indwelling power of Christ. To fret over the concept of the "straight" and "narrow" way and that fact that most will not find it is enough to inspire the purveyors of smooth doctrines. The text does not refer exclusively to unbelievers. Christians often want to claim the promises of God without adhering to His requirements; they prefer a dream over reality. Herein rests the source of a weak or confused faith and worse, a subtle renunciation of the gospel charter.

"Go ye therefore, and teach all nations, baptizing them in the name of the Father, and of the Son, and of the Holy Ghost: Teaching them to observe all things whatsoever I have commanded you: and, lo, I am with you always, even unto the end of the world. Amen" (Matt. 28:19, 20).

In the book of Revelation, God makes a special plea:

"And I heard another voice from heaven, saying, Come out of her, my people, that ye be not partakers of her sins, and that ye receive not of her plagues" (Rev. 18:4).

Any good student of the Bible will tell you, Revelation is no place to begin a sermon or lecture to the unlearned or for that matter to most who consider themselves Christian. Although the final book of prophecy is intriguing even to secularists, the very fact that people try to unravel its mysteries without first understanding the basics is why there is so much pop-culture interpretation. However, not difficult to glean from this particular text are two elements that will get us started—"come out" and "my people."

In every country, city, and town, in every village, barrio, caste, and class, and inside the multitude of churches, God has His elect by faith. They have different styles of worship in numerous denominations. Some are missionaries in remote places on foreign soil and others in their own communities. Nevertheless, the Bible tells us that not everyone is where the Lord wants them. But is this a geographical or a spiritual misplacement? Revelation 18:4 is both a plea and a warning. Before we can understand either one, we must know toward whom the Lord directs them. We saw earlier that not everyone who proclaims themselves a Christian is worthy. Who exactly then are God's true people? From where is the angel telling them to come out? What sins are they in danger of enjoining if they stay? Finally, and most important of all, how can I tell if it's me?

Chapter 2
"My People"

*But this thing commanded I them, saying, Obey my voice, and I
will be your God, and ye shall be my people: and walk ye in all the ways that
I have commanded you, that it may be well unto you.*
Jeremiah 7:22

Since the beginning, there have been two classes: there is one class made up of people who lovingly and joyfully submit to the will of God and another which does not. One class recognizes their need for a Savior and one does not. We might automatically assume these two categories differentiate the believer from the non-believer. To a certain extent that is absolutely true, but I must point out that neither Cain nor Abel was an atheist. The classification of God's true people comes down to something more than belief.

Some will say we cannot lump everyone into one category or the other; we must allow for the possibility that there are people who fall somewhere in the middle, and God will not hold them accountable for what they do not know; we have to realize that some people are not aware that they need a Savior or what it actually means to submit themselves to God. Is it fair to classify the merely ignorant with the clearly obstinate? Cannot one conduct their lives in such a way that is good and decent, outside any need or knowledge of God? This latter point is the rationale of the non-believer, and as thoughtful as these arguments sound, all fall short of addressing the point. Though a person may have the perception that ignoring the truth is an option with no consequences, they are aware that the choice exists, which means they are not wholly ignorant. That is why there is evangelism—to explain why a person cannot remain in a perpetual state of indecision because, eventually, everyone afforded the choice must decide.

Yes, there are people who pass away without a clear understanding of the gospel. There are people struck down, especially children, who never had the opportunity to learn about Jesus. While some churches teach concepts to deal with these kinds of cases, it is more appropriate (and more correct) to leave those judgments in the hands of God. Our purpose here is not to address the "what ifs."

Until God rejected Cain's method of tribute, an offering which literally comprised the fruits of his own labor, Cain thought the Lord should number him in the class with Abel. When Cain murdered his brother in response to that rejection, it proved to everyone in which category he belonged. The story of Cain and Abel does not languish in the past. Its message is at the crux of the point in Matthew 7:21–23, and it is a lesson that applies today.

Every denomination will assert that they are among the Lord's elect, usually at the exclusion of all others. Unfortunately, like Cain, many people presume to offer the Lord what they believe He would respect and honor as a token of worship, but there is the terrible possibility that one might make the same mistake that Cain did.

The distinguishing feature between one church and another is their doctrines, and even within a particular sect there are variations. But dogma is not the measure of faith, and the Bible makes no mention of a preference for any particular church based on a set of beliefs. God uses another gauge to determine who His people are.

"And the LORD hath avouched thee this day to be his peculiar people, as he hath promised thee, and that thou shouldest keep all his commandments" (Deut. 26:18).

"The LORD shall establish thee an holy people unto himself, as he hath sworn unto thee, if thou shalt keep the commandments of the LORD thy God, and walk in his ways" (Deut. 28:9).

"By this we know that we love the children of God, when we love God, and keep his commandments. For this is the love of God, that we keep his commandments: and his commandments are not grievous" (1 John 5:2, 3).

"Here is the patience of the saints: here are they that keep the commandments of God, and the faith of Jesus" (Rev. 14:12).

Faith is a relationship with God. That relationship engenders love, trust, and the surrender of our will through obedience. While we are only saved by grace through faith in Christ and not our knowledge of the Bible, false doctrine can damage that relationship.

The simplicity of the texts above is unmistakable. The pride of individuality among many churches causes a preference for error to overshadow these basic concepts. Some denominations believe Christ nailed the commandments to the cross. Others say that obedience is so utterly impossible that it is pointless and even sinful to try, and a recently introduced doctrine teaches that God's love prevails in the end to the extent that God will save everyone, dead or alive, regardless of their Christian experience. We will elaborate on these errors as we continue. The point we want to demonstrate here is that these three false doctrines, while they sound appealing, utterly contradict the texts above and it does not take a "real expert" to help us understand this fact.

In the book of Revelation, chapters 2 and 3, the Lord both chastens and encourages seven separate churches, each named for the city in which they reside. Although the Lord extols many of their virtues, He also condemns everything from hypocrisy and ambivalence to apostasy and false teaching. In each case He reinforces the importance of repentance and the outcome for those who are able to gain the victory over sin. He makes that especially clear to the last church, Laodicea, which represents the bulk of God's people at the time of the end. They have become so comfortable and self-assured in their lifestyles and religion that they have utterly lost sight of their need for Christ. However, the Lord does not praise even one of these churches on the basis of a unique set of beliefs or religious practices.

"And he that overcometh, and keepeth my works unto the end, to him will I give power over the nations" (Rev. 2:26).

"He that overcometh, the same shall be clothed in white raiment; and I will not blot out his name out of the book of life, but I will confess his name before my Father, and before his angels" (Rev. 3:5).

"Him that overcometh will I make a pillar in the temple of my God, and he shall go no more out: and I will write upon him the name of my God, and the name of the city of my God, which is new Jerusalem, which cometh down out of heaven from my God: and I will write upon him my new name" (Rev. 3:12).

"To him that overcometh will I grant to sit with me in my throne, even as I also overcame, and am set down with my Father in his throne" (Rev. 3:21).

It may seem that the information presented so far runs contrary to my original premise and that I am downplaying the significance of doctrine. I ask my readers to bear with me. The point we endeavor to stress here is that our ability to overcome is imperiled by a lack of knowledge, but it is not guaranteed by what we do know.

> *Faith is not a mere emotional response or a feeling; it is bound to sincere acts of repentance, compassion, and self-sacrifice for the benefit of others, even those who hate us.*

Some churches correctly assert that all we must do is love God and one another. However, they tragically disassociate God's commandments from how we demonstrate that kind of love. Faith is not a mere emotional response or a feeling; it is bound to sincere acts of repentance, compassion, and self-sacrifice for the benefit of others, even those who hate us. No deed, no words, no thought that runs counter to the commandments is an act of love.

The portion of the law, which Jesus voided, was ceremonial in nature—animal sacrifices, daily atonement rituals, a rigorous schedule of religious observances, and the feast days. In the old covenant, these practices symbolized the redemptive work of our High Priest, Jesus Christ. Each generation of Jews drilled in the ceremonies that would ultimately convey to the world the true meaning of the sanctuary and the manner in which God would free humanity from their slavery to sin. With His sacrifice, Jesus, the Lamb of God, ended the need for the ritual ordinances. But the moral law, which is unchangeable, remains as an eternal testament to God's character and the unwavering standard by which He judges man.

"Master, which is the great commandment in the law? Jesus said unto him, Thou shalt love the Lord thy God with all thy heart, and with all thy soul, and with all thy mind. This is the first and great commandment. And the second is like unto it, Thou shalt love thy neighbour as thyself. On these two commandments hang all the law and the prophets" (Matt. 22:36-40).

The first four commandments govern our walk with God, and the latter six governs our relationship to other people. They are not mutually exclusive. We cannot love our fellow man (or God), if we disrespect our parents, kill, commit adultery, steal, lie, or covet. Similarly, what becomes of our commitment to God if we hold something else in higher esteem? Money, fame, fashion, food, entertainment, and even our bodies can become forms of idolatry. Along with worldly distractions, using the

Lord's name with irreverence and neglecting to keep the Sabbath holy also prove that our affections lie elsewhere. We cannot express the depth of the meaning to God's law in a single paragraph, but Christ conveyed the rationale for obeying it in one small sentence: "If ye love me, keep my commandments" (John 14:15).

Many people view Christianity in the context of weekly church attendance while others spread that definition even thinner by proclaiming their faith just once or twice a year. Church affiliation does not define a believer at heart, only in appearance. Moreover, those who view obedience in the strict confines of refraining from public acts that cross the bounds of the Decalogue assume they walk in harmony with the divine mandate. The Pharisees thought the same way and made a deliberate show of their outward religiosity. However, Jesus pointed out that sin begins in secret, buried in the deep recesses of the heart whether it precedes an overt act or not. Truly, a Godly and loving obedience must engender this concept for every commandment.

A lesson we might take away from the letters to the seven churches is that God does have people in many denominations. However, in every church there must exist the same fundamental understanding of His doctrine—obedience to the commandments is repentance! Without this vital effort to improve in our Christian walk, our relationship with God is not what it should be.

Some churches draw a distinction between our "reward" and the promise of eternal life. They say Jesus guarantees the believer a seat at the royal banquet by what He did at the cross and the reward is a bonus, i.e. more jewels in the crown, an elevated status in heaven, a better parking space, etc. This is all while teaching that sinning until Jesus comes is unavoidable, a forgone conclusion, and without any eternal consequences. My friends, what incentive is there for repentance if one believes there is nothing they can do to lose their salvation? What kind of faith will they manifest? The concept of guaranteed salvation does not agree with the message to the seven churches, and it leads nearly anyone who believes it to the broad path of destruction.

"Remember therefore from whence thou art fallen, and repent, and do the first works; or else I will come unto thee quickly, and will remove thy candlestick out of his place, except thou repent" (Rev. 2:5).

"He that hath an ear, let him hear what the Spirit saith unto the churches; He that overcometh shall not be hurt of the second death" (Rev. 2:11).

"Repent; or else I will come unto thee quickly, and will fight against them with the sword of my mouth" (Rev. 2:16).

"Remember therefore how thou hast received and heard, and hold fast, and repent. If therefore thou shalt not watch, I will come on thee as a thief, and thou shalt not know what hour I will come upon thee" (Rev. 3:3).

"As many as I love, I rebuke and chasten: be zealous therefore, and repent" (Rev. 3:19).

"He that hath an ear, let him hear what the Spirit saith unto the churches" (Rev. 3:22).

Victory depends upon the sincerity of our desire to change. The Lord does not force us to surrender. He wants us to agree to abide by His will because we love Him, because of the sacrifice He made for us, and because sin separates us from Him. We do not obey God to earn ourselves a place in heaven. Our acts of righteousness are not good enough and when performed out of expectation of reward, they are entirely self-serving. Salvation comes only by grace through faith, and without faith, it is impossible to please God (see Heb. 11:6). We should take comfort in the fact that we do not work for our salvation, but that our good works are the emblems of our sanctification, the symbols of our faith.

> *Victory depends upon the sincerity of our desire to change.*

"For, brethren, ye have been called unto liberty; only use not liberty for an occasion to the flesh, but by love serve one another" (Gal. 5:13).

Through prayer and submission, the Holy Spirit gives us the knowledge and the strength we need during the battle between the spirit and the flesh—the struggle with self. Christ's victory over the flesh does not give man license to continue in sin. We must believe that through the atoning blood of His Son, symbolized by the Old Testament sacrifices, God forgives us for the sins of our past.

"Being justified freely by his grace through the redemption that is in Christ Jesus: Whom God hath set forth to be a propitiation through faith in his blood, to declare his righteousness for the remission of sins that are past, through the forbearance of God; To declare, I say, at this time his righteousness: that he might be just, and the justifier of him which believeth in Jesus" (Rom. 3:24–26).

Jesus lived a holy and righteous life, but Christ could have chosen to sin. Had he done so, the entire human race would be lost. The cross did not end the battle over sin; it gave us the most potent weapon of all: the miracle of Christ in us. All true Christians must face the inner warfare between the flesh and the spirit. This is the wonder of true Christianity; human beings have been given the right and the means to leverage the power of the living God to gain the victory in this battle.

People begin to stumble because of the potential for sin in the future. Those who believe we cannot refrain from sin, and thus need not try, harbor a fundamental misunderstanding of the gospel. It is true that the grace of God means that we now rely on the righteousness of Christ to cover our sins. He pleads His blood before the Father on our behalf; He is our intercessor. However, it is a great misconception and even greater false teaching that tells us that victory over sin is unnecessary and impossible. With God, all things are possible (see Matt. 19:26 and Luke 18:27). In our own strength, we will fail; in Christ's, we prevail.

The loving, free-will conformity of our lives to the revealed will of God is the measure of our faith, and without faith, it is impossible to please God. Surrendering to God proves whether we appreciate the sacrifice Jesus made to merit our justification in the eyes of God. But, more than that, surrendering cannot happen unless we cooperate with the Holy Spirit and pray for a complete conversion. The battle with self is different for each person, and this is what makes Jesus our personal savior. When we allow Jesus into our lives, we start to live in the manner He wants us to. Our thoughts and desires change, bad habits begin to disappear, and a love for others begins to blossom. We are new creatures, but this does not mean that surrendering comes easily. It takes constant vigilance and prayer to stay connected with God.

Our own righteousness can never be enough to save us. It is faith in Christ's victory over sin that covers our transgressions. Nonetheless, we strive toward that mark of Christ's character because Jesus died to make our salvation possible. The justification of man was something only the blood of the Lamb could accomplish because without it, our case was hopeless.

As we said, many think the death of Jesus is both the beginning and the end of the new covenant. Some teach that Christ accomplished His entire work at the cross and that man bears no further responsibility for his eternal destiny. The thief on the cross may not have had long to repent, but repent he did. His sincere confession of guilt and plea for mercy in the presence of the Savior proved him worthy of paradise. Had he chosen not to humble himself before Christ, the Savior's death would have done nothing for him.

So long as the breath of life is in our lungs, sanctification is a continual process. We cannot plan for a death bed conversion to prepare our characters for heaven. If we know the truth now, we must strive to live it now. If we reject the voice of the Holy Spirit or delay submission to it long enough, our justification runs the risk of becoming meaningless and void.

> *The cross did not end the battle over sin; it gave us the most potent weapon of all: the miracle of Christ in us.*

How do we hear the Holy Spirit? He is that small voice in our conscience, which tells us right from wrong, good from bad, what to do and what not to do. Every time we make a decision that goes against the divine council found in the Bible, we grieve the Spirit of God. The conviction of sin grows less and less with each repetition; the heart hardens, until finally, we hear nothing and feel no sense of remorse for sin at all. This is the gravest of all conditions for the Christian, more dangerous even than the ignorance of unbelief.

"And grieve not the holy Spirit of God, whereby ye are sealed unto the day of redemption" (Eph. 4:30).

"For it is impossible for those who were once enlightened, and have tasted of the heavenly gift, and were made partakers of the Holy Ghost, And have tasted the good word of God, and the powers of the world to come, If they shall fall away, to renew them again unto repentance; seeing they crucify to themselves the Son of God afresh, and put him to an open shame" (Heb. 6:4–6).

"Wherefore I say unto you, All manner of sin and blasphemy shall be forgiven unto men: but the blasphemy against the Holy Ghost shall not be forgiven unto men" (Matt. 12:31).

Man is not free to sin and expect no consequence, whether those consequences manifest in the temporal world or not. Eternal loss is just as much a choice as eternal life. God preselected all men for salvation, but we must choose to accept the requirements. The freedom we find in the gospel is not freedom from responsibility; it is freedom from the slavery of sin and our fallen nature. When we make the choice to follow God, it comes with a daily and lifetime commitment to walk the narrow path of sanctification. This is the faith of Jesus and of all His true followers. Anything else is mere lip-service.

Chapter 3
Crucial Realities and Common Sense

But the natural man receiveth not the things of the Spirit of God: for they are foolishness unto him: neither can he know them, because they are spiritually discerned.
1 Corinthians 2:14

Discernment, according the Merriam-Webster dictionary, is the quality of being able to grasp and comprehend what is obscure. No one would deny that many biblical concepts fit the definition of obscure. Misunderstandings are inevitable when one does not recognize the need for discernment.

Few of us would enter a darkened room in a building we were unfamiliar with, that is, without a source of light. The risks to those who would are quite obvious. Nothing quickens the spirit more effectively than stepping on a cat's tail. When we do have the wisdom to pack a flashlight, a kerosene lamp or even a candle, we must also be cognizant of the fact that those tools require a source of energy. Batteries need a charge, a candle must have ample wax, and a lamp must have fuel.

For many, when one first opens the scriptures and begins to read, it is as if they are walking into that dark and unfamiliar building with dead batteries. They can discern almost nothing. One understands most of the words without comprehending any of the passage. In the King James Version, the use of old world expressions can exacerbate the problem. Unfortunately, this often leads to frustration for some and reluctance to go any further. For others, it can lead to assumptions. They perceive a path with no obstacles, and as they push further into the dark, it becomes that much harder for them to find a way out.

The Word of God is a source of light in a sin-darkened world, but it does no one any good if they neglect the fuel source that makes it shine, the Holy Spirit. Praying for guidance is essential to understand the concepts presented in scripture. Without this divine assistance, many interpretations will inevitably suffer the error of human ideas. This chapter contains several examples of concepts that many understand in the wisdom of men. We will demonstrate with help from the Spirit and some plain old logic how the Bible wants us to understand them.

With a fresh understanding of some fundamentals from the previous chapter, let us review our opening verse from Revelation 18 and add two more to establish the context around this warning.

"And after these things I saw another angel come down from heaven, having great power; and the earth was lightened with his glory. And he cried mightily with a strong voice, saying, Babylon the great is fallen, is fallen, and is become the habitation of devils, and the hold of every foul spirit, and a cage of every unclean and hateful bird" (Rev. 18:1, 2).

"And I heard another voice from heaven, saying, Come out of her, my people, that ye be not partakers of her sins, and that ye receive not of her plagues" (Rev. 18:4).

Obviously, the actual city of Babylon no longer exists. Thus, the reference is not strictly geographical. This is our first example of discernment. Many have looked for a temporal reconstruction of Babylon in some form to fulfill this prophecy. In Jeremiah 51:62 and 64, the Bible says that Babylon will remain desolate forever and not rise again. How then are we to comprehend what Revelation 18 is actually talking about? Why is Babylon fallen? What are her sins? First, we need a little historical background.

Revelation refers to Babylon in order to lead us back to the Old Testament to search out her example and relevance to prophecy. The Lady of Kingdoms was a pagan empire, given wholly to idolatry, mysticism, sorcery, and a host of other godless practices. Her influence and subjugation of the Jewish people led many of them into the same sins (see Ezek. 23). Although she had logged centuries of false worship and heathen rituals, it was the desecration of God's holy temple, during the reign of King Belshazzar, which finally brought about her demise (see Dan. 5).

"The voice of them that flee and escape out of the land of Babylon, to declare in Zion the vengeance of the LORD our God, the vengeance of his temple" (Jer. 50:28)

"For Israel hath not been forsaken, nor Judah of his God, of the LORD of hosts; though their land was filled with sin against the Holy One of Israel. Flee out of the midst of Babylon, and deliver every man his soul: be not cut off in her iniquity; for this is the time of the LORD's vengeance; he will render unto her a recompence. Babylon hath been a golden cup in the LORD's hand, that made all the earth drunken: the nations have drunken of her wine; therefore the nations are mad" (Jer. 51:5-7).

The content of the warning in Jeremiah 51:6 is identical to the one given in Revelation 18. For seventy years, Babylon held the Jews captive by the will of God for Israel's transgressions. With that time of correction fulfilled, the cup of the Lord's indignation toward the Chaldeans had run over. The Jews' liberation was at hand.

"And, behold, here cometh a chariot of men, with a couple of horsemen. And he answered and said, Babylon is fallen, is fallen; and all the graven images of her gods he hath broken unto the ground" (Isa. 21:9).

We turn now to the Babylon of Revelation 18 where the parallels are striking. Although it may be that Baal worship and graven images are spiritual relics of the past, many of the motivations behind modern false worship are hardly different. Historically, when men do not accept the requirements of God, they have looked for ways to reorder their worship to appease themselves.

Jesus warned His followers about the coming of deceivers, phony messiahs, and wolves in sheep's clothing. In Romans 1, Paul taught about those who "hold the truth in unrighteousness"; he spoke about "deceitful workers" and "false apostles" in 1 Corinthians 11; and he spoke about "those having a form of godliness, but denying the power thereof" in 2 Timothy.

In 1 and 2 John, the apostle writes this about a character known as the antichrist.

"Little children, it is the last time: and as ye have heard that antichrist shall come, even now are there many antichrists; whereby we know that it is the last time" (1 John 2:18).

"Who is a liar but he that denieth that Jesus is the Christ? He is antichrist, that denieth the Father and the Son" (1 John 2:22).

"And every spirit that confesseth not that Jesus Christ is come in the flesh is not of God: and this is that spirit of antichrist, whereof ye have heard that it should come; and even now already is it in the world" (1 John 4:3).

"For many deceivers are entered into the world, who confess not that Jesus Christ is come in the flesh. This is a deceiver and an antichrist" (2 John 7).

Sensationalized by Hollywood and fiction writers alike, many people look for the antichrist as a dastardly character of highly unsavory traits. If the antichrist were such a person, would he really be that difficult to spot? John points out that anyone who denies the nature of Jesus has this character. But what John describes is not an overt and obvious dispute with Christianity. It is not atheism; it is a deception.

In John's day a theological error known as Gnosticism claimed that Christ, being sinless, could have had no part in humanity because of the allegedly inherent evil of everything that is not spiritual, most notably the flesh. The Gnostics did not deny Christ's existence; instead, they surmised that He existed on a higher level. Some even claimed that Jesus was a ghost. In whatever form they thought he came in, their doctrine conveyed the notion that Jesus had no need to overcome temptation because He was not flesh, and thus, he could not sin. The Gnostics lumped themselves into this same category of spiritual elitism and declared that they were also above any requirement for repentance.

The mystery of Christ, the union of divinity and humanity, is something no one can fully comprehend or explain. However, the mere fact that Jesus stated unequivocally that He had overcome the world, testifies to the potential fallibility of His flesh and blood nature. He was tempted, He was tried, and He very well could have stumbled. His victory over human imperfection is fundamental to Christianity, and His life was the model for walking the narrow path. Had he been incapable of falling into sin, the same as any human, His example would have been pointless.

"For we have not an high priest which cannot be touched with the feeling of our infirmities; but was in all points tempted like as we are, yet without sin" (Heb. 4:15).

The term, antichrist, does not mean the opposite of Christ; it refers to one who opposes or takes the place of, without initially appearing to. This is a crucial distinction because therein rests the deception. Could what John describes be the negative-counterpart to the Lord and still go undetected by the masses? Who would he fool? Did the philosophies or goals of Hitler or Saddam Hussein, two men that some claim were the antichrist, attempt to fly under the religious radar? Did they deceive anyone spiritually? Clearly not; their lofty aspirations bore no relevance to religion, Christian or otherwise. Is the antichrist a pompous proponent of humanism, one who proudly trumpets the quintessential doctrine of ignorance—evolutionism? Will they hold the truth in unrighteousness? No, they will not hold the truth at all.

There is an important difference between an unbeliever or spiritual antagonist and the antichrist. Atheists are not false apostles; they do not peddle a counterfeit gospel. They are in error, but they deceive no one. However, as John describes, the antichrist will.

"Little children, it is the last time: and as ye have heard that antichrist shall come, even now are there many antichrists; whereby we know that it is the last time. They went out from us, but they were not of us; for if they had been of us, they would no doubt have continued with us: but they went out, that they might be made manifest that they were not all of us" (1 John 2:18, 19).

Christ referred to Judas as the "son of perdition" in John 17:12. The only other biblical reference to use that expression applies to "that man of sin" in 2 Thessalonians 2:3. Judas, the forerunner of the antichrist, was not an unbeliever; he was a professed follower. Although he did not have a clear understanding of the Messiah's mission and Christ did not choose him directly, he mingled with Christ's inner circle and laid claim to the discipleship. The Bible proves decisively that the antichrist is not the polar opposite of Jesus, but one who denies the Lord implicitly and seeks to exalt himself from within just as Judas did.

"Let no man deceive you by any means: for that day shall not come, except there come a falling away first, and that man of sin be revealed, the son of perdition; Who opposeth and exalteth himself above all that is called God, or that is worshipped; so that he as God sitteth in the temple of God, shewing himself that he is God" (2 Thess. 2:3, 4)

An atheist might rail all day long against the truth. They can flail against the historical facts with circular logic and feckless rhetoric. They can claim Christ did nothing apart from give eloquent speeches, but in so doing, they are simply wrong and pull the wool over no one's eyes, especially the Christian.

Let me digress for a moment to address my agnostic readers. Forget about the limits of your imagination or the human rationales that make one question what no one can completely fathom. God exists, He loves you, and He sent His Son to die for you so that He could bring you home. What do I or any true Christian have to gain by spreading the gospel if it were not true? The apostles certainly garnered nothing from the world by their efforts except persecution. But what we do obtain from the truth is peace, the realization that there is something more to life than death, and the knowledge that we are right with our Father in heaven. This peace is not a self-actuated understanding of life gained through a vacuous human philosophy of "enlightenment," ideas which come from dead men. This peace comes by the power of the living God! Christ fills the void caused by loneliness; He washes away the sadness and despair brought about by sin. He causes us to rejoice in a newness of heart and revel in a freedom from our fallen condition that nothing else can match. To appreciate and even comprehend this experience, one must be willing to allow the Spirit of God into their heart. One must be open to the miracle of God in us.

To one extent or another everyone looks for meaning to their existence. The world offers only temporary fixes, many of which cannot outlast the rigors of aging and others which are utterly pointless and self-destructive. In the gospel we find no greater joy or more important purpose than serving God, not merely by going to church every weekend, but through selfless acts of compassion, ministering to the economically poor as well as the poor in spirit, comforting the physically or socially afflicted, and sharing the testimony of scripture. Yet, there is another purpose to Christianity that transcends the good works we perform here on earth.

Few people ever learn about or consider the significance of humanity beyond what we perceive in our tiny sphere of influence. A person once conveyed to me their concept of God and His regard for man in this way: if there is a God, she said, He created the whole universe, and He does not care if one tiny planet believes in Him or not. She has it half right—He did create the whole universe. However, not only does the Lord care deeply for each and every one of us, He has chosen the heart of man as the proving ground for the integrity of His government and the wisdom of His judgment.

The first to rebel against the government of God was Lucifer. The greatest of all created beings, this mighty angel, the covering cherub, would not accept the notion that he should submit to any Lordship. His great pride would eventually spur an uprising that cost heaven a third of its angels.

"How art thou fallen from heaven, O Lucifer, son of the morning! how art thou cut down to the ground, which didst weaken the nations! For thou hast said in thine heart, I will ascend into heaven, I will exalt my throne above the stars of God: I will sit also upon the mount of the congregation, in the sides of the north: I will ascend above the heights of the clouds; I will be like the most High" (Isa. 14:12–14)

"And there appeared another wonder in heaven; and behold a great red dragon, having seven heads and ten horns, and seven crowns upon his heads. And his tail drew the third part of the stars of heaven..." (Rev. 12:3, 4).

"And there was war in heaven: Michael and his angels fought against the dragon; and the dragon fought and his angels, And prevailed not; neither was their place found any more in heaven" (Rev. 12:7, 8).

The exile of Lucifer to the earth, where he became known as Satan and the devil, did not end the conflict. The enemy persisted in his accusations, insisting that sentient beings would never love a God who ruled over them. See for yourself how he addresses the King of the universe when dealing with the condition of fallen man:

"And the Lord said unto Satan, Hast thou considered my servant Job, that there is none like him in the earth, a perfect and an upright man, one that feareth God, and escheweth evil? Then Satan answered the Lord, and said, Doth Job fear God for nought? Hast not thou made an hedge about him, and about his house, and about all that he hath on every side? thou hast blessed the work of his hands, and his substance is increased in the land. But put forth thine hand now, and touch all that he hath, and he will curse thee to thy face" (Job 1:8–11).

Satan predicted that Job's sorrow over the loss of family, possessions, and his own health would destroy his respect for God. He surmised that men would view their afflictions as punishment for sin and should, in the devil's mind, consider the Lord a tyrant. Although Job did express his bewilderment over those trials, what we find throughout his book is a heartfelt search for the answers to his affliction. He questioned God, but he did not curse Him. Job did not spend his time wondering how he was going to replace his livestock. Ultimately, Job learned a few things about himself and a great deal more about God. In the end the blessings he received exceeded everything previously known, and the devil had been proven wrong. Unfortunately, for many people today, it would appear that Satan might have had a point.

This has been the great drama throughout history—the enemy is seeking to ruin man by poisoning his relationship with God. As Christians, we bear witness to the character of the Lord before the universe. The devil stands as our accuser, asserting that we should not be accounted worthy of heaven because we are sinners. It would seem that Satan does not understand the concept of reconciliation.

Sending Jesus to die for us proves the love of God. Accepting His sacrifice as atonement for our sins proves the grace of God. Providing us the means of sanctification through the Word proves his wisdom, and allowing the life

> *This has been the great drama throughout history—the enemy is seeking to ruin man by poisoning his relationship with God.*

we lead in Christ to vindicate His name proves the judgment of God. That is our calling, our most profound purpose in life, to exalt the name of Jehovah and rejoice in the blessing of being made in the image of the Almighty.

"For I think that God hath set forth us the apostles last, as it were appointed to death: for we are made a spectacle unto the world, and to angels, and to men" (1 Cor. 4:9).

We return now to our study of the antichrist. John's warning is about those who " … went out from us, but they were not of us … " an overt naysayer would never originate from within the body of believers. The antichrist emerges from among the discipleship, not to deny Christ openly, but by claiming he is a follower while simultaneously harboring a doctrine that denies the truth about Jesus. This is what makes the antichrist so deceptive and so very dangerous.

How does any of this relate to the Babylon of Revelation? The reference to this ancient city is cryptic for a purpose—so that the wise will take time to study it. Pagan Babylon sets the spiritual precedent for the symbolism in end-time prophecy. Her activities, especially those that led Israel astray, are the paradigm for the warning at the core of our discussion.

Unfortunately, as with many things difficult to understand in scripture, diverse interpretations have emerged, which have only confused and contorted the truth. For example, one interpretation of prophecy examines history no further than the latter half of the first century. Known as preterism, this belief asserts that the Babylonian reference in Revelation only applies to the past, specifically to Israel! Preterists cite as evidence the apostasy of the Jewish state during the interim between the crucifixion of Christ and destruction of Jerusalem by the Romans in AD 70. The Jews continued in the defunct practices of the old covenant after Christ's death, and because of their unbelief, the Lord declared their temple desolate and void. It was because of the temple desecration that Babylon fell to the Medes. Circumstantially, this may seem somewhat helpful to the doctrine of preterism, which explains why the error is common.

In the gospels of Matthew, Mark and Luke, Jesus foretold of the peril to those living in Jerusalem in its last days. However, it was a warning for His first century followers and for the true church at time of the end (see Matt. 24:3). He told them to watch for the sign that it was time to leave.

"And when ye shall see Jerusalem compassed with armies, then know that the desolation thereof is nigh. Then let them which are in Judaea flee to the mountains; and let them which are in the midst of it depart out; and let not them that are in the countries enter thereinto" (Luke 21:20, 21).

This warning came not because Jerusalem in the latter days of the first century represented the New Testament Babylon, but rather because a pagan empire of the same ilk, Rome, was about to invade. Some believe the city's destruction was the final fulfillment of the last-days prophecy spoken by Christ in Matthew 24, Mark 13, and Luke 21. They submit that Nero, who met his demise in AD 68 and who was responsible for the persecution of thousands of new believers, was the antichrist. There is no doubt that Nero was not a big fan of Christians, but he lacked the deceptive nature inherent to the character of which John wrote. Nero made no pretense of faith, he did not come out from among the discipleship, and he offered no theological contradictions to the nature of Christ; he was simply a murderer. This is another example of how we must use discernment in our interpretations.

The prophecies Jesus spoke about in the gospels had a dual application. First, it applied to the siege against Jerusalem, which would raze the temple to the ground, and second, it dealt with the end of the world. Moreover, John wrote the book of Revelation between AD 90 and 95. This is at least twenty years after the fall of Jerusalem to the Romans. If the symbolism relevant to Babylon ended with the demise of the first century Jewish state, why would the Lord inspire John to write a warning to flee the city more than two decades after the fact? This is just common sense!

Lastly, preterism finds its adherents split over the most obvious shortcoming of the concept ... the reality of the second coming of Jesus, which the Bible says will be as visible as His ascent into heaven (see Acts 1:11). If Bible prophecy concludes in the first century, what becomes of this inarguably seminal event? Preterists have convenient and superficially plausible explanations. Notably, they say that Christ's second coming was strictly spiritual; it was the kingdom of God in us through baptism of the Holy Ghost. While this may sound viable, it is not in agreement with the Bible. The gift of the Holy Spirit cannot be the final act of prophecy; it is not Christ's second advent. Even among preterists there is disagreement with their doctrine—a portion believing in a literal second advent and another faction adhering to the strictly spiritual interpretation.

Finally, there is another concept, prevalent among evangelicals and widely depicted by some fiction writers. This idea forestalls nearly all of the New Testament prophecy, some citing timeframes upwards of a thousand years from now. It is appropriately called futurism. The belief incorporates doctrines such as the secret rapture and a forthcoming antichrist. With such disparate understandings, we have a prime example of confusion—the transliteration of Babel, forerunner of ancient Babylon, and the very essence of the kingdom described in Revelation 18. However, as we will learn, there is more happening inside Babylon than mere error.

Although the Old Testament attributes the spiritual infidelity of the Jews to their excursions into paganism—the worship of Babylonian idols—nowhere in scripture does the abominations of Babylon ever symbolize the spiritual adultery of Israel. Why would the Bible start doing so in Revelation? In fact, the only New Testament references to Babylon, used outside of Revelation, refers to Rome (see 1 Peter 5:13), the preeminent pagan empire of John's day. It was the idolatry and spiritualism of the Chaldeans that corrupted Israel. This is the key to understanding what the Lady of Kingdoms represents, both long ago and in the present day. Finally, theologies that limit this crucial reference to Israel's sordid past overlook Babylon's most notable characteristic—global control and influence. From Revelation 17, we read this:

"And upon her forehead was a name written, MYSTERY, BABYLON THE GREAT, THE MOTHER OF HARLOTS AND ABOMINATIONS OF THE EARTH … And the woman which thou sawest is that great city, which reigneth over the kings of the earth" (Rev. 17:5, 18).

Spiritually, Babylon's machinations were and are the most corruptive and controlling influence in the world. On the other hand, Israel never controlled anything, temporally or spiritually. In the New Testament, Israel represents something other than the community of literal Jews. What is the reality of Israel since the death of Christ? What is a Jew under the new covenant?

"There is neither Jew nor Greek, there is neither bond nor free, there is neither male nor female: for ye are all one in Christ Jesus. And if ye be Christ's, then are ye Abraham's seed, and heirs according to the promise" (Gal. 3:28, 29).

"That at that time ye were without Christ, being aliens from the commonwealth of Israel, and strangers from the covenants of promise, having no hope, and without God in the world: But now in Christ Jesus ye who sometimes were far off are made nigh by the blood of Christ" (Eph. 2:12, 13).

Today, Israel is subject of much false teaching, which leads many Christians to believe prophecy and even their salvation hinges on the fortunes of a tiny country in the Middle East. Biblical texts that describe the judgment of those who would wage war on Israel are not referring to literal military campaigns in the last days. This is where so many have their spiritual focus diverted. While we can stand shoulder to shoulder with the only democracy in the region and confront the tyrannical regimes surrounding her, the eternal destiny of Christians does not rely upon that temporal outcome. The judgment of end time persecutors of Israel refers to anyone who rejects Christ by virtue of attacking his church, his people, spiritually or otherwise. Literal Israel stumbled over Christ and fulfilled the prophecy Jesus cited from the Old Testament.

"And he shall be for a sanctuary; but for a stone of stumbling and for a rock of offence to both the houses of Israel, for a gin and for a snare to the inhabitants of Jerusalem. And many among them shall stumble, and fall, and be broken, and be snared, and be taken" (Isa. 8:14, 15).

"The stone which the builders refused is become the head stone of the corner" (Ps. 118:22).

"Jesus saith unto them, Did ye never read in the scriptures, The stone which the builders rejected, the same is become the head of the corner: this is the Lord's doing, and it is marvellous in our eyes? Therefore say I unto you, The kingdom of God shall be taken from you, and given to a nation bringing forth the fruits thereof" (Matt. 21:42, 43).

As a state, literal Israel lost its corporate status as the chosen people with their rejection of Christ and the new covenant, but God did not forsake the Jews. For three and one-half years after the Savior's death, the apostles worked tirelessly to bring the gospel to their Jewish brethren. They too, as individuals, could accept the grace of God just as any Gentile does. Paul, speaking about his countrymen, said this:

"Brethren, my heart's desire and prayer to God for Israel is, that they might be saved. For I bear them record that they have a zeal of God, but not according to knowledge. For they being ignorant of God's righteousness, and going about to establish their own righteousness, have not submitted themselves unto the righteousness of God. For Christ is the end of the law for righteousness to every one that believeth" (Rom. 10:1–4).

Let us briefly deviate away to explain Romans 10:4. Jesus did not curtail the moral portion of the law. The word "end" means purpose or goal, such as in the common phrase—"the end justifies the means." The "end" of the law is to demonstrate our need for Christ. The law shows us our woeful condition, for sin is the transgression of the law (see 1 John 3:4). We need Jesus because the law cannot change, and it cannot save us. Most of the Jews never understood this concept. They trusted in a legalistic approach to honoring God and believed their outward appearance of righteousness would earn them His favor. Nevertheless, repentance and a change of heart has always been what God wanted from men.

"And Samuel said, Hath the Lord as great delight in burnt offerings and sacrifices, as in obeying the voice of the Lord? Behold, to obey is better than sacrifice, and to hearken than the fat of rams" (1 Sam. 15:22).

"For I desired mercy, and not sacrifice; and the knowledge of God more than burnt offerings" (Hosea 6:6).

Many Christians have gone to the opposite extreme by believing that the covenant of grace voids the law entirely. This is simply not true. When a police officer lets a speeder off with a warning, it is an act of grace, but the law still exists. The motorist is not free to speed again. If he does and the same officer stops him a second time, could the driver claim innocence to a judge because he thought he was under grace? Think carefully and prayerfully about that.

Israel, in the spiritual sense, is still a nation of peculiar people and a royal priesthood. Christians of all races are now the Jews of the new covenant, the elect of God by faith not by blood. All are welcomed into the citizenship of Israel by grace through faith in Jesus Christ. What the Old Testament symbolized in historical events became the spiritual reality of the New. The problem is that many people who now believe the New Jerusalem is their inheritance stake their claim to the kingdom in another place: a place of fables, smooth doctrines, and religious confusion—the city of spiritual Babylon.

Chapter 4
Been There, Done That—How History Reveals Prophecy

The thing that hath been, it is that which shall be; and that which is done is that which shall be done: and there is no new thing under the sun.
Ecclesiastes 1:9

Biblical prophecy did not conclude in the first century. The book of Daniel, the gospels, many of the epistles, and especially the book of Revelation all contain historical waymarks that are discernible only to those who take the time to study them and allow conviction by the Holy Spirit. For our purposes, revealing the fullness of those prophecies and the extent of Babylon's transgressions goes well beyond the scope of this book. Ultimately, what we hope for you to see is the reality of spiritual Babylon rather than explore every facet of her chicanery. This will help those with hearts open to the truth to determine whether they are among the people God has called to come out. However, we must render at least a portion of Babylon's history and her transgressions because therein rests confirmation of this truth.

"For all nations have drunk of the wine of the wrath of her fornication, and the kings of the earth have committed fornication with her, and the merchants of the earth are waxed rich through the abundance of her delicacies" (Rev. 18:3).

Revelation receives much acclaim as a literary masterpiece. The symbolism in chapter 18 gives us a sampling of Babylon's malicious behavior in John's creative and truly inspired prose. Drunk with wine, vengeful, fornicating with kings and spiritual profiteering, Babylon is a busy lady. What does all this mean?

The "abundance of her delicacies" refers to teachings that appeal to the religious palate but provide no nourishment for the soul. This is the spiritual junk food Babylon markets to expand her influence. Just as many in the world suffer poor health due to an over indulgence in rich, fatty and utterly worthless food, the purveyors of smooth and delicious doctrine have prospered on the global demand for transcendental cupcakes and deep-fried religion. No matter how pleasant they are to eat, they are nothing but harmful to the body of Christ.

These descriptions of spiritual Babylon impress me to reinforce an important point; the object of God's complaint is not the faithful trapped within her. The plea to His people is to avoid being caught up in her sins and partaking of her unhealthy fare. He wants them to spiritually flee in order to escape the judgment that will ultimately bring Babylon down forever.

John's imagery is obviously metaphorical and like most of Revelation, we must go back to the Old Testament to understand the example. The most basic concept of understanding Bible prophecy is that the temporal often symbolizes the spiritual. The nature of future events finds its basis in the past. In John 5:39, Jesus said about the scriptures "…that ye think ye have eternal life: and they are they which testify of me." The book of Isaiah, for example, makes many clear prophetic references to Christ and only Christ could have fulfilled them.

"Surely he hath borne our griefs, and carried our sorrows: yet we did esteem him stricken, smitten of God, and afflicted. But he was wounded for our transgressions, he was bruised for our iniquities: the chastisement of our peace was upon him; and with his stripes we are healed" (Isa. 53:4, 5).

The parallels between the history of Israel and the life of Jesus demonstrate this past–future relationship beyond what many people realize. For instance, a man named Joseph brought Israel into Egypt to escape a famine. It was another Joseph who took the infant Jesus to Egypt to escape a famine of human misery caused by Herod. Jacob, renamed Israel by the Lord, fathered twelve sons who were the patriarchs of the twelve Jewish tribes; Jesus chose twelve apostles who seeded a nation of spiritual Jews, Christianity. Israel endured forty years of purification in the wilderness; Jesus endured forty days.

When God handed down the commandments at Mount Sinai it was the first time many had ever heard the law, yet none of what God said was new. The Bible says Abraham obeyed God's laws and ordinances (Gen. 26:5). The fourth commandment tells us to "remember the Sabbath" (Exod. 20:8). God wrote the law in stone at Mount Sinai to demonstrate its eternal nature and so men would not forget it a second time. Jesus spoke the law at the Mount of Olives so men would finally understand it.

Multiple prophets predicted the seventy-year captivity of the Jews. It happened. The book of Daniel foretells the demise of ancient Babylon at the hand of Medes and Persians. History records that event. Daniel wrote that the Greeks would conquer the Persians some 200 years before it occurred. Alexander the Great fulfilled that prophecy. The Bible predicted the rise of Pagan Rome and their role in the crucifixion of Christ. Both happened. Scripture confirmed the foresight of God by showing us how to calculate the start of Christ's ministry in AD 27 and His death in AD 31. It also gives a starting point from which to mark the countdown … 490 years before.

As we alluded earlier, the cryptic nature of prophecy demands careful and diligent study. However, its complexity does not give a student license to apply their personal interpretation and make assumptions about its meaning. For example, the following verse receives much attention from secular prognosticators and the church alike.

"And the sixth angel poured out his vial upon the great river Euphrates; and the water thereof was dried up, that the way of the kings of the east might be prepared" (Rev. 16:12).

There are many who propose that this text describes the prelude to a massive military incursion aimed at Israel. They assume the aggressor is an Asiatic nation primarily because the text refers to the east. The obvious presumption is that the Bible must refer here to the Far East. Is that really what it means? When one examines the immediate context of this verse, they will see how the Bible wants them to interpret this verse.

First, if one believes this text refers to a modern armed invasion in the traditional sense, one must use literal observations to explain it. Why would a contemporary military force need to drain a river before they launch an attack? Don't planes and missiles fly? Second, simple geography tells us the Euphrates River is hundreds of miles from the Jewish homeland. It would not realistically factor into any strategy for an actual invasion of Israel.

There are many texts in the Bible that are allegorical and many that are literal. When properly studied, the Bible makes the interpretation for us. In order to understand a text, we refer to the past and to the greater context of any given passage.

Historically, the conquest of ancient Babylon did occur with a very similar event. The Euphrates River ran under and through the great kingdom. The army of the Medes and Persians, the kings of the east, could not breach the city walls. However, they cleverly surmised that if they diverted the Euphrates, they could march beneath the walls, into the interior, using the dry river bed. The Medes accomplished this feat, and Babylon fell to them in a single night.

The historical precedent indicates that the event spoken of in Revelation applies to Babylon, not Jerusalem, and since the actual city no longer exists, the reference is clearly figurative. Lastly, the drying up of the Euphrates is the sixth of the seven last plagues. Israel is not the recipient of God's wrath; spiritual Babylon is.

Now that we have demonstrated what Revelation 16:12 does not mean, how do we interpret what it does mean? The Bible gives us answers. Not only is Babylon a symbolic reference throughout Revelation, the water on which she sits is one as well.

"And there came one of the seven angels which had the seven vials, and talked with me, saying unto me, Come hither; I will shew unto thee the judgment of the great whore that sitteth upon many waters" (Rev. 17:1).

"And he saith unto me, The waters which thou sawest, where the whore sitteth, are peoples, and multitudes, and nations, and tongues" (Rev. 17:15).

The Euphrates sustained life in Babylon. It was the city's greatest natural asset and her only vulnerability. In the spiritual sense, modern Babylon receives support from her waters too, the people. Revelation 17:15 identifies the water in this prophecy as multitudes from many nations. The sixth plague "dries up" that support, which in turn prepares the way for the kings from the east. The Bible does not specifically state how the sixth plague accomplishes this feat. Although scripture tells us the end result, it will not always provide the details that get us to that point. This can lead men to seek answers regarding those mysteries where prophecy is silent, but they run the risk of error, sometimes with devastating consequences. The literal interpretation we spoke about above fuels the doctrines, which focus Christian eyes on the Middle East. Although it is hard to overlook the ominous rhetoric and violence coming from nations surrounding Israel, we can only stress that the biblical threat is global, not regional, and that spiritual Jews in the new covenant, whom are also spread out across the planet, are the seed of Abraham by faith, not by flesh.

"That is, They which are the children of the flesh, these are not the children of God: but the children of the promise are counted for the seed" (Rom. 9:8).

"And if ye be Christ's, then are ye Abraham's seed, and heirs according to the promise" (Gal. 3:29).

Finally, we come to the kings of the east. Is this a reference to Russia, China, or perhaps Iran, once called Persia? Obviously, since Babylon does not physically exist, no country can invade it. When Saddam Hussein thought to rebuild the city, futurists were giddy with anticipation because they thought it was a prelude to the fulfillment of prophecy. Had they bothered to study the biblical account from Jeremiah 51, they would have learned that Babylon would never rise again in the temporal sense. Her destruction was total and permanent. The destiny of her spiritual counterpart will be exactly the same (see Rev. 18).

Some use the specious and bigoted claim that the Jews run the world financially and pull all the political strings. They believe this is the measure of Babylon's influence. Does this idea match her description in prophecy? On the contrary, money and power, though worshipped by many people, are not the abominations that trap the unsuspecting. We must always remember the Bible's spiritual framework. Secular high-finance does not qualify as literal false worship. Revelation's use of the term "kings" implies something other than an army of earthly conquerors. Who are the kings of the east? There is a definite answer:

"And, behold, the glory of the God of Israel came from the way of the east: and his voice was like a noise of many waters: and the earth shined with his glory" (Ezek. 43:2).

"For as the lightning cometh out of the east, and shineth even unto the west; so shall also the coming of the Son of man be" (Matt. 24:27).

"And the armies which were in heaven followed him upon white horses, clothed in fine linen, white and clean ... And he hath on his vesture and on his thigh a name written, KING OF KINGS, AND LORD OF LORDS" (Rev. 19:14, 16).

The interpretation of prophecy does not need speculation, but the requisite for understanding is still discernment. We examine the context of a passage, identify the biblical precedent, apply some logic, and finally, allow the Bible to make the interpretation for us. Does this mean we can answer every question that might arise and will every answer satisfy? Sadly, for many, the answer is no. Understanding Revelation requires a level of conviction that can only come with the aid of the Holy Spirit. This is why it is so important to pray for guidance before one undertakes a sincere study of scripture. To carry the truth in one's heart requires divine installation.

The unbelieving world, which cannot understand the truth, rejects the biblical answers. They look for scientific or psychologically appealing explanations for everything, and many churches go along with them in order to appease their own doubts and pacify their detractors. Nevertheless, we study so that we need not make assumptions. History testifies to the veracity of Bible prophecy. Thus, because the Word is demonstrably accurate about the future, as proven by the past, we have unswerving confidence in its inspired nature and no reason to doubt the spiritual events to come.

"Now faith is the substance of things hoped for, the evidence of things not seen" (Heb. 11:1).

"Knowing this first, that no prophecy of the scripture is of any private interpretation. For the prophecy came not in old time by the will of man: but holy men of God spake as they were moved by the Holy Ghost" (2 Peter 1:20, 21).

Unfortunately, the world and many churches perceive prophecy in the likeness of fortunetelling. Sadly, they miss the greater point. Not every vision or dream came to a prophet with a clear-cut explanation. In fact, the Bible states that there were some prophecies no one would comprehend until men had the opportunity to look back through time and see how history was revealed in scripture before it happened.

"And I heard, but I understood not: then said I, O my Lord, what shall be the end of these things? And he said, Go thy way, Daniel: for the words are closed up and sealed till the time of the end" (Dan. 12:8, 9).

The point is: God wants us to realize He is the One who knows the end from the beginning. The fulfillment of prophecy is not as much about knowing the future as it is to build trust and faith that what God tells us is true. Scripture did not say how the Greeks would conquer the Persians. The vision given to Daniel merely said it would occur swiftly and that Greece would split into four kingdoms soon thereafter. It was not until after Alexander the Great had accomplished that feat only to die suddenly, which led to the Macedonian empire's four way division among his generals, that anyone could decipher the vision. This is how prophecy unfolds. We cannot know all the mysteries by which the Lord works. But God does tell us the end, so that when it comes to pass, it inspires confidence and trust, which strengthens our belief.

"And now I have told you before it come to pass, that, when it is come to pass, ye might believe" (John 14:29).

It is a sad, but certain fact that many churches misrepresent some portion of the gospel. Clearly, such a statement puts the burden of proof on this writer. Some believe that diversity of beliefs lends itself to the richness of the Christian faith. This is only true to the extent that a particular emphasis on doctrine harmonizes with scripture. There can be only one Christian theology at the foundation and that doctrine must be Christ's. A church may focus its teachings on repentance, another on missionary work, and a third to explaining prophecy, but these three are intertwined and inseparable. The effort to put forth to accomplish all three (and more) is part and parcel of Christian unity. At the heart of the matter, unity of the faith is a heart like Christ's.

When a church teaches the gospel or prophecy in such a way that its people do not gain a proper understanding of repentance or good works, that church is not in harmony with Christ. What is worse than ignorance is the deliberate watering-down of doctrine in the name of expedience. Modern religion is not immune to the allurements of the world, the desire for profit, influence and even power. Although not all churches have fallen into such temptation, every house of worship has the same basic need—to grow their congregation. This has led to grievous compromises on many beliefs, but the biggest compromise is most decidedly on the very foundation of Christianity itself—the six days of Creation.

Historically, the emergence of diverse denominations, which resulted from the 16th century Protestant reformation, was largely due to a preference (or disagreement) people developed for a certain ecclesiastical style or teaching. The trend continues to this day. Mainstream churches dilute their original canon and permit worldliness to mingle with holiness in order to attract new converts, stem the tide of declining membership, or to appease secular critics. Some members find themselves bewildered by these discrepancies. New churches form in the wake of disputes, and the basis of their doctrine is often not about reform, but the placation of wants and fears.

Finally, at the root of the problem for spiritual Babylon is the truth itself. The Bible conveys the knowledge and wisdom we need to find the one and only path to eternal life, Jesus Christ. With a pure and unwavering heart, we must choose to follow Him. The enemy works to prevent us, and he is often successful.

One of the most insidious deceptions of them all is the idea that we can keep one foot in the world and the other on the narrow way. In other words, some think we can have our sinful cake and eat it too. Obviously, the Bible conveys no such concept, but many churches do. A fundamental truth that is often rejected is that we cannot divide our interests. "Thou shalt have no other gods before me" (Exod. 20:3). People have many gods in a world filled with questionable entertainment and ample avenues for self-indulgence. Fidelity to the Creator is a vital component of the Christian walk under constant assault by a sin-infested world. These distractions, though notoriously effective, are only a part of Satan's line of attack; he uses another avenue to seek the overthrow of one's faith—sophistry, the believable lie.

The enemy revealed his most enduring strategy in the Garden of Eden. Obviously tempted by the prospect of obtaining knowledge and wisdom, it was Satan's suggestion that God was not being completely honest with her that made Eve cross the line. Sophistry, a lie painted with a thin coating of truth, are like drops of poison in the water of life and are the most effective means to steer people to the path of destruction. To this day the devil still encourages men to presume upon the will of God instead of understanding it as it is written. His success rate is staggering. When humans reject the Word, they imagine solutions for their problems and concerns, but they are not the right answers according to our biblical knowledge.

The Old Testament Jews were as religious as they came. However, observe what Paul said about their religious experience: "For I bear them record that they have a zeal of God, but not according to knowledge" (Rom. 10:2). Similarly, many Christians have a zeal for God, but their doctrines are based on flawed foundations and human rationales. Exploiting fear and ignorance, the enemy, through the doctrines of Spiritual Babylon, convinces millions that their eternal destiny is bound to the consumption of bread and wine, depends upon third-party (human) absolution, is earned by works, genealogically predetermined, guaranteed by baptism, requires no repentance, is gained by monetary contributions, or finally, requires only a verbal profession of faith. These are just some of the major errors that plague the Christian world. Welcome to the state of religious confusion; welcome to spiritual Babylon.

Purposeful or not, there is more to the problem than doctrinal error. Indeed, if misunderstandings in liturgy and dogma were truly innocent, correction might be a simple matter. Babylon's sins run much deeper.

"Babylon hath been a golden cup in the LORD's hand, that made all the earth drunken: the nations have drunken of her wine; therefore the nations are mad" (Jer. 51:7).

The Bible is not suggesting that the entire planet liquored up at a Babylonian keg party. Wine or strong drink, though sometimes included in calls for sobriety, also refers metaphorically to the deleterious effects of bad doctrine. Here is proof.

"For their rock is not as our Rock, even our enemies themselves being judges. For their vine is of the vine of Sodom, and of the fields of Gomorrah: their grapes are grapes of gall, their clusters are bitter: Their wine is the poison of dragons, and the cruel venom of asps" (Deut. 32:31, 32).

Stay yourselves, and wonder; cry ye out, and cry: they are drunken, but not with wine; they stagger, but not with strong drink. For the LORD hath poured out upon you the spirit of deep sleep, and hath closed your eyes: the prophets and your rulers, the seers hath he covered" (Isaiah 29:9, 10).

The drunkenness of the world results from partaking in the wine of Babylon. With the help of satanic agents, she brews, ages, and bottles the deceptions that blind men from the truth. The allegory of intoxication represents the majority of the world's inability to comprehend the truth from a spiritual stupor. Deuteronomy 32:31 reveals the most telling fact of all about the "Rock" whom those that drink the dragon's poison have denied:

"The LORD is my rock, and my fortress, and my deliverer; my God, my strength, in whom I will trust; my buckler, and the horn of my salvation, and my high tower" (Ps. 18:2).

"For who is God save the LORD? or who is a rock save our God" (Ps. 18:31).

"The LORD liveth; and blessed be my rock; and let the God of my salvation be exalted" (Ps. 18:46).

Whether by virtue of idolatry or advocating a version of the gospel that does edify the body of Christ, any doctrine that fails to point people to the Lord, our Rock, is a recipe for disaster. However, just as errors wrought by ignorance are not the extent of religious confusion, deceptions are also not the limit of Babylon's abominations.

Chapter 5
Religious Persecution– A Historical Legacy

Yea, and all that will live godly in Christ Jesus shall suffer persecution.
2 Timothy 3:12

Apostasy in some form has been a problem in every age of man. Had that been the extent of Babylon's transgressions, it would make her more difficult to set apart for recognition. The Bible assigns this "woman" two more distinguishing features—wrath and fornication. These two traits, above all others, help one to identify their spiritual captor. What is Babylon angry about and how or with whom does she commit fornication? While many character traits have a symbolic meaning, the wrath of Babylon is quite literal, and it has a specific target. Let us examine our historical precedents.

Cain was the first to set a standard for religious persecution. From what we can tell in his story, the only gripe he had with Abel was his method of worship and not receiving the Lord's blessing. Abel's offering and its approval from God angered Cain who felt his fruit basket or veggie platter was just as worthy. Cain's conviction of guilt came from within, but he blamed it on his brother.

With very few exceptions, most of the prophets sent by God to straighten out the people were not well received. Elijah, Isaiah, Jeremiah, and then later John the Baptist, each of the apostles, and of course, Jesus, all suffered the wrath of kings. There is one story though, from the Old Testament, which sets our standard for the wrath of Babylon.

"Nebuchadnezzar the king made an image of gold, whose height was threescore cubits, and the breadth thereof six cubits: he set it up in the plain of Dura, in the province of Babylon....

Then an herald cried aloud, To you it is commanded, O people, nations, and languages, That at what time ye hear the sound of the cornet, flute, harp, sackbut, psaltery, dulcimer, and all kinds of music, ye fall down and worship the golden image that Nebuchadnezzar the king hath set up:

And whoso falleth not down and worshippeth shall the same hour be cast into the midst of a burning fiery furnace" (Dan. 3:1, 4-6).

The king of Babylon erected a great image of gold and commanded that everyone must bow down and worship the image or suffer a death sentence. We soon discover that there were a few who refused to bow even in the face of such a threat. But before we reveal who balked at the king's demand, let us point out some important and enlightening characteristics of this environment.

One must wonder why the king built such an image in the first place. In chapter two of Daniel, Nebuchadnezzar had a dream where a great statue reflected the current preeminence of Babylon. The dream also included the rise of successor nations and the eventual demise of the kingdom. However, what captivated the Nebuchadnezzar most was the part that fed his ego, the head of gold, which represented his reign.

"And wheresoever the children of men dwell, the beasts of the field and the fowls of the heaven hath he given into thine hand, and hath made thee ruler over them all. Thou art this head of gold" (Dan. 2:38).

Rather than take the dream's interpretation to heart and try to learn why Babylon would eventually fall, the king chose to thumb his nose at the prophecy. He built an image fashioned entirely of gold thereby declaring the perpetuity of his kingdom. He rejected the message given to him through Daniel and placed his own judgment and aspirations above that of God.

With that backdrop, let us examine the scenario in Daniel 3. Nebuchadnezzar was a state leader. He had no spiritual credentials. Although God allowed him to attain a lofty position and even used him as a rod of correction upon the Jews, he did not have divine authority to establish and enforce any sort of worship, especially of an idol. This obvious fact did not escape the three men who refused to kneel.

"Wherefore at that time certain Chaldeans came near, and accused the Jews. They spake and said to the king Nebuchadnezzar, O king, live for ever. Thou, O king, hast made a decree, that every man that shall hear the sound of the cornet, flute, harp, sackbut, psaltery, and dulcimer, and all kinds of music, shall fall down and worship the golden image: And whoso falleth not down and worshippeth, that he should be cast into the midst of a burning fiery furnace. There are certain Jews whom thou hast set over the affairs of the province of Babylon, Shadrach, Meshach, and Abednego; these men, O king, have not regarded thee: they serve not thy gods, nor worship the golden image which thou hast set up. Then Nebuchadnezzar in his rage and fury commanded to bring Shadrach, Meshach, and Abednego. Then they brought these men before the king" (Dan. 3:8–13).

Notice the sort of reverence proffered to Nebuchadnezzar in verse 9. The servants clearly regarded the king with a god–like veneration as they delivered some bad news: not everyone was willing to bow before the image. Obstinate in his eyes, these righteous men became the target of the king's wrath. Although their disobedience agitated Nebuchadnezzar, he gave Shadrach, Meshach, and Abednego one more chance to "repent."

"Nebuchadnezzar spake and said unto them, Is it true, O Shadrach, Meshach, and Abednego, do not ye serve my gods, nor worship the golden image which I have set up?

Now if ye be ready that at what time ye hear the sound of the cornet, flute, harp, sackbut, psaltery, and dulcimer, and all kinds of music, ye fall down and worship the image which I have made; well: but if ye worship not, ye shall be cast the same hour into the midst of a burning fiery furnace; and who is that God that shall deliver you out of my hands?" (Dan. 3:14, 15).

The three brave Jews stood their ground. They rejected the king's offer, opting to place their trust in God's ability to deliver them from the death decree. Notable here is the absence of presumption on the part of these men.

"Shadrach, Meshach, and Abednego, answered and said to the king, O Nebuchadnezzar, we are not careful to answer thee in this matter. If it be so, our God whom we serve is able to deliver us from the burning fiery furnace, and he will deliver us out of thine hand, O king. But if not, be it known unto thee, O king, that we will not serve thy gods, nor worship the golden image which thou hast set up" (Dan. 3:16–19).

They displayed faith and profound bravery by refusing to bow before the image, knowing that God could protect them but not assuming that He would. Either way, by sacrifice or survival, God would deliver them. This is a quintessential example of faith in the face of persecution. Not moved by their loyalty to God, Nebuchadnezzar becomes even angrier. He pronounces the death sentence, and the king's executioners cast the three men alive into a superheated furnace.

"Then was Nebuchadnezzar full of fury, and the form of his visage was changed against Shadrach, Meshach, and Abednego: therefore he spake, and commanded that they should heat the furnace one seven times more than it was wont to be heated. And he commanded the mostmighty men that were in his army to bind Shadrach, Meshach, and Abednego, and to cast them into the burning fiery furnace. Then these men were bound in their coats, their hosen, and their hats, and their other garments, and were cast into the midst of the burning fiery furnace" (Dan. 3:19–21).

God preserved these faithful men from harm and destroyed their would-be executioners. Although this story has a relatively happy ending for the three Jews, the suitably impressed king still did not quite grasp the concept of free-will in regards to worship. Nebuchadnezzar issues a final decree, which punished anyone for speaking a word against the God of the Jews.

The image erected by the state and the enforcement of worship in literal Babylon sets the stage for the scenario to unfold in spiritual Babylon. Just as the death decree fell upon those who would not bow before the image on the plain of Dura, so too will the wrath of modern Babylon come upon those who will not yield to the decrees that she too will make. The coming pages will reveal the nature of the image she raises and the decree to worship.

Nebuchadnezzar attempted to merge his power as head of state with a presumed right to dictate the practice of paganism. He united government and religion in the institution of false worship and pronounced capital punishment for all who disobeyed. In this instance, the three men, each faithful to the point of death and defiant of the king's decree, became the enemy of both church and state.

Spiritual Babylon adds a new dimension to her transgressions, which is considered the liaison between her and the kings of the earth. In other words she is in bed with states and governments, which means she has integrated herself into the leadership of the entire world. Prophecy labels Babylon the "Great Whore" in Revelation 17. This undoubtedly stems from that improper relationship and refers to "fornication" in conjunction with wrath. The metaphor describes an affair conceived in hostility for a common enemy. What is the source of this anger? How does this collaboration and hostility manifest in world events?

Recall Revelation 16:12, where the angel pours out the sixth plague to dry up the Euphrates River. We noted that this event signifies the evaporation or removal of Babylon's support. Now notice the verse that immediately follows as well as verse 19, which aids in interpretation.

"And the sixth angel poured out his vial upon the great river Euphrates; and the water thereof was dried up, that the way of the kings of the east might be prepared. And I saw three unclean spirits like frogs come out of the mouth of the dragon, and out of the mouth of the beast, and out of the mouth of the false prophet.... And the great city was divided into three parts, and the cities of the nations fell: and great Babylon came in remembrance before God, to give unto her the cup of the wine of the fierceness of his wrath" (Rev. 16:12, 13, 19).

The Bible tells us there are three parts to Babylon—the beast, the false prophet, and the dragon. What does each of these represent? The symbolism is complex. This is why the Bible says in 2 Timothy 2:15, "Study to show thyself approved unto God, a workman that needeth not to be ashamed, rightly dividing the word of truth." I encourage my readers to hang in there. This subject is not only deep; it is extremely important. The enemy seeks to discourage your pursuit of knowledge, but the Lord promises a blessing to all those who read and understand this message.

"Behold, I come quickly: blessed is he that keepeth the sayings of the prophecy of this book" (Rev. 22:7).

I cannot understate the significance of these three entities, historically and spiritually. When the sixth plague causes Babylon to lose her support (see Rev. 16:12), the world will see a surge in efforts to deceive the people (see Rev. 16:13). Like the frogs that overran Egypt during the ten plagues, Babylon's abominations will infest every quarter of society. The beast, the false prophet, and the dragon spew the doctrines of a counterfeit religious system, a form of Christianity that deceives. When people finally start realizing the truth, they will flee the system in droves. This spiritual evacuation constitutes the drying up of the Euphrates. Babylon, however, will not give up her captives without a fight, and many will remain loyal.

> *When the sixth plague causes Babylon to lose her support, the world will see a surge in efforts to deceive the people*

"For they are the spirits of devils, working miracles, which go forth unto the kings of the earth and of the whole world, to gather them to the battle of that great day of God Almighty" (Rev. 16:14).

Babylon will step up the battle with miracles of satanic power. She will reinforce the delusions that enslaved people from the start. The target of her wrath and the reason for her fornication with kings will be to gather the world against the source of her consternation. The battle against God is the final attempt to eradicate the truly faithful, the people who will not kneel before the beast's image. It will be her strongest effort to destroy those who preach, teach, and live out the real, everlasting gospel. Once again, there is Old Testament prophecy and historical proof to validate this coming event.

"I considered the horns, and, behold, there came up among them another little horn, before whom there were three of the first horns plucked up by the roots: and, behold, in this horn were eyes like the eyes of man, and a mouth speaking great things" (Dan. 7:8).

"I beheld, and the same horn made war with the saints, and prevailed against them" (Dan. 7:21).

"And he shall speak great words against the most High, and shall wear out the saints of the most High, and think to change times and laws: and they shall be given into his hand until a time and times and the dividing of time" (Dan. 7:25).

Contrary to what many think, a saint is not a person set aside for canonization after having lived a storied life. No selection committee or panel of human judges determines if ones character is worthy of exaltation. If that were the definition of a saint, meaning that they are already in the grave, how could the little horn make war against them? The Bible defines a saint:

"To all that be in Rome, beloved of God, called to be saints: Grace to you and peace from God our Father, and the Lord Jesus Christ" (Rom. 1:7).

"Unto the church of God which is at Corinth, to them that are sanctified in Christ Jesus, called to be saints, with all that in every place call upon the name of Jesus Christ our Lord, both theirs and ours" (1 Cor. 1:2).

"Here is the patience of the saints: here are they that keep the commandments of God, and the faith of Jesus" (Revelation 14:12).

Daniel 7 tells us that many who are obedient to God would one day see themselves persecuted by the little horn. Why, though? The little horn thinks to change God's laws and alter the prophetic timeline (see Dan. 7:25). How could a man do that? He cannot. The Bible says he thinks to. The distinction means that the Little Horn makes others believe prophecy occurs differently than scripture foretells and that he has the ability (and the right) to modify the Ten Commandments. The persecution will occur because the saints, God's true followers, will not assent to these changes nor will they recognize any man's authority to make them. This is exactly the position of the three men who defied Nebuchadnezzar.

"And when he had opened the fifth seal, I saw under the altar the souls of them that were slain for the word of God, and for the testimony which they held" (Rev. 6:9).

The first identifying trait of the little horn is words spoken against the most high or blasphemy. The most notable example of such an offense is the attempt to appropriate the dominion of God. How do we know the little horn is not merely a reference to some notorious atheist? There have been many despots and godless persecutors of the saints. However, a non-believer would never claim to have the divine power and authority they deny. An atheist not only scoffs at the existence of a God, they reject the concept of sin or any need for atonement. That is foolishness, but it is not blasphemy. The little horn is not a proclaimed atheist. On the contrary, the words he speaks against the Most High are not to deny the Lord but to put himself in God's place. That is the definition of blasphemy, and a bit later we shall uncover the literal manifestation of this affront to God, which exists in modern Babylon.

Now we come to the second of little horn's abominations. Consider this: if the holy law could change, Jesus had no need to die. His sacrifice was necessary precisely because the commandments are as unchangeable and eternal as God himself. The commandments define sin. If they no longer apply or if Christ voided them, why do we still need a Savior? Jesus did not end the law nor did He eliminate our vulnerability or susceptibility to future sin. Christ did what only the blood of the Son of God could do; He provided the atonement necessary for man's justification. Sin is still transgression of the law. All who reject this truth and claim that Christ nailed the Ten Commandments to the cross or that a man has the power to change it are operating under a delusion.

Chapter 6
He Shall Think to Change the Times ...

And he said unto them, It is not for you to know the times or the seasons,
which the Father hath put in his own power.
Acts 1:6

The enemy has a multitude of ways of causing men to rationalize a decision and not hear or understand the words of God. I implore my readers to listen to the still, small voice as you read. You may feel pangs of anxiety if something does not match your understanding. I also once struggled with certain truths and looked for passages in the Bible to alleviate my concerns, but that is not the correct way to study scripture. The Word of God was not inspired for the purpose of validating man's ideas. It is to convey to us the mind of God; it is meant to help us understand His character and His concept of love.

The prophecy of Daniel 7:25 says that the little horn thinks to change the "times." Obviously, this is impossible. However, making people believe the prophetic timeline is something other than what the Bible teaches is not impossible. This is especially true when the falsehood is appealing. The Bible has a prime example.

Among the Jews living in Christ's time, most thought the Messiah's mission was to break the chains of their Roman oppressors and restore their nation to its former glory. Even after His resurrection, many Jews continued to believe that Jesus would reign on a temporal throne.

"When they therefore were come together, they asked of him, saying, Lord, wilt thou at this time restore again the kingdom to Israel?" (Acts 1:6).

Clearly someone taught them wrong. As a consequence, many Israelites who grew up faithful to their understanding of the old covenant missed out on the most profound spiritual blessing of freedom from the bondage of sin and the promise of eternal life, which are clearly offered in the new covenant.

For anyone to think a similar error like the one committed by the Jews could never happen to a Christian is both naïve and dangerous. We see it all the time in failed attempts to predict the date, time, and nature of Christ's return. This unfortunate error, when its folly becomes apparent, results in spiritual doubt and encourages open ridicule of one's faith. Sadly, one can easily avoid this mistake. The Bible says no one knows when Christ will return, that only God the Father knows (see Matt. 24:36). There are signs that time is getting short, but it is a mistake to predict the day.

Another mischaracterization of the times is known as the secret rapture. This nineteenth century concept teaches that Christians will not have to endure end time events because Jesus will whisk us off to heaven prior to the pouring out of God's wrath. Where is the biblical precedent for that? There is none. In fact, the opposite is true. Israel was in Egypt during the ten plagues. God preserved and protected the Jews, and the final few afflictions fell only upon the Egyptians … but the Lord did not beam the Jews off to Canaan. Jesus warned believers of the time to flee Jerusalem before the Roman assault, but there was no miraculous rescue. Christians were to recognize the warning signs for themselves.

But the modern rapture concept holds out an even fatter carrot for the marginal believer; it gives the incentive of a second chance. Some say those left behind have the opportunity to rethink their opinion of Jesus as their Savior. The doctrine submits that some not taken to heaven on the first try would find themselves stranded on earth for seven additional years and have that period to reinvest in the truth and prove their faith. After which, the doctrine alleges, Christ comes again, visibly this time, and fetches the rest of His rehabilitated flock.

Beloved, even if one does not subscribe to the notion of a second chance, persecution is still a foregone conclusion for believers in the last days. Trials and tribulation will separate the nominal Christian from the true. When churches teach otherwise, they inspire a faith that is tepid. The Lord does not abide in a wait-and-see attitude. Though He once winked at the times of the ignorant, He calls us all to repentance now. If one doubts before the Lord comes, they will not have the luxury of changing their mind after and expect the same honor as those who believed without seeing!

"That the trial of your faith, being much more precious than of gold that perisheth, though it be tried with fire, might be found unto praise and honour and glory at the appearing of Jesus Christ" (1 Peter 1:7).

Biblically, the secret rapture is a simple matter to debunk. Matthew 24 stresses that end time events occur under the same spiritual circumstances that were present during the time before the flood. For 120 years, the antediluvians would not heed Noah's preaching to repent and take refuge in the ark. When the flood waters finally came, it swept them all away. They were left to die without a second chance to reconsider their choice.

Nevertheless, the rapture concept puts millions at ease because either they do not know the truth or because they will not accept it. It is not my purpose to scare people. Though fear is a powerful motivator, love is even better. Jesus will come again to gather His faithful, but only once. He created us for His good pleasure and paid the ransom for our redemption with His own blood. He will not let us remain on this sin-stricken planet forever. His greatest desire is to commune with the people He created, loves, and died for. Is the gift of eternal life not worth any sacrifice we might have to make in order to honor what Jesus did for us?

The Bible says only the Father knows when the second coming will occur. The secret rapture concept starts a countdown to the visible event. This fundamentally contradicts Matthew 24:36: "But of that day and hour knoweth no man, no, not the angels of heaven, but my Father only."

If one haggles over the fact that the text refers only to the day and the hour but makes no mention of the year, they are missing the point. Jesus tells us what to watch for, to know the time of the end is nearing. The day remains a mystery, so that men will not think they can bide their time, delay repentance, and postpone their sanctification.

"For he saith, I have heard thee in a time accepted, and in the day of salvation have I succoured thee: behold, now is the accepted time; behold, now is the day of salvation" (2 Cor. 6:2). This is why the Lord tells us to be ready now because the day, which comes as a thief in the night, is a surprise and a shock to the unprepared, but it is a joyous occasion for those who watch for the signs.

"But the day of the Lord will come as a thief in the night; in the which the heavens shall pass away with a great noise, and the elements shall melt with fervent heat, the earth also and the works that are therein shall be burned up" (2 Peter 3:10).

"Behold, he cometh with clouds; and every eye shall see him, and they also which pierced him: and all kindreds of the earth shall wail because of him. Even so, Amen" (Rev. 1:7).

There will be no secret evacuation of the church. The second coming is bold, fiery, and witnessed by the entire world. It comes with the voice of the archangel and the trumpet of God. The Bible uses the metaphorical reference to a "thief" in the same immediate context as the boisterous end of the world, so there really isn't anything stealthy about it. The Bible also makes no intimation that the text applies to two separate instances of Christ's return, one in secret and another overt. The metaphor only means that one must be spiritually prepared for the arrival of Jesus.

Some use the rapture terminology simply to identify the "appearance" of Christ. This is apart from the concept of a covert rescue mission and does not preclude end time persecution for the faithful. We should not confuse the two practices. However, we will refrain from using the word in this context so as to avoid that problem or give a measure of credibility to the rapture fable.

Perpetrated largely by the Pharisees and the Sadducees, the error foisted on the Israelites was a terrible tragedy. The purveyors of false doctrines in much of modern Christianity replay and expound upon the old mistakes, while they add many new ones. Those who teach doctrines such as the secret rapture, once saved always saved, or genealogical predestination, do much damage to gospel fundamentals such as repentance, sanctification, and a free will acceptance of the truth. Offering prayers for our dearly departed, for example, not only does nothing for the dead, it sends the wrong message to the living. It tells them someone else will bear the burden for their redemption after they have passed away. It gives one a reason to hedge their bets in life and gamble on their chances in death. Doctrines such as these supplant the truth. They are a part of the spiritual confusion that typifies Babylon. However, the ministers of these faiths seldom claim the mantle of Christ as their own, but the little horn goes to that extreme.

"Let no man deceive you by any means: for that day shall not come, except there come a falling away first, and that man of sin be revealed, the son of perdition; Who opposeth and exalteth himself above all that is called God, or that is worshipped; so that he as God sitteth in the temple of God, shewing himself that he is God" (2 Thess. 2:3, 4).

We must ask ourselves, why would anyone want to do this? Prophecy may be mysterious and cryptic, but it is also certain that God meant for us to understand it, and He assured Daniel that we would in the future. Now, why does the little horn try to change the meaning of the times? Suppose someone, through a careful study of history and prophecy, figured out who the little horn was? Clearly, the party responsible for blasphemy severe enough to warrant a record of it in scripture would not want the public to know the Bible was talking about them. One of three things must occur: they would have to repent with strong apologies, make vehement denials, or they could deflect attention away from the evidence and away from themselves. The little horn chose the latter tactic.

We previously mentioned two opposing methods of biblical interpretation: preterism and futurism. To reiterate, the first concept teaches prophetic completion in the first century with the exception of the second coming. The second idea submits the notion that Revelation depicts events that occur largely in the future. Hence, those people continue to anticipate the coming of the antichrist in spite of the fact that such a philosophy existed even in John's day. Clearly, these two theories, which largely ignore the history in between them, cannot both be right. So, which one is? Or, is neither of them? Which half of these believers is deceived, or are both?

Many Protestants, Evangelicals, and other denominations adhere to one or the other of these two concepts. Ironically, neither idea emerged from within those churches. The fact is that both ideas sprang from the same source. Preterism and futurism are doctrines promoted by Francisco Ribera, Luis De Alcazar, and Cardinal Robert Bellarmine. These men are all members of the Jesuit priesthood. These doctrines found their way into the mainstream Christian thinking at the direction of the Roman Catholic Papacy.

I hear the groans and moans already. There it is—another book on the verge of bashing Catholics! No, my friends, nothing could be further from the truth. This is not about the faith or faithfulness of individual believers. It is about a system that misleads you. For some, even a suggestion of that possibility is preposterous.

This may come as small consolation to those of you who already feel insulted or angry at the direction this book is taking. But before you throw this book in the trash can, please consider some things. For centuries, the papal system had manipulated and coerced the rulers of Europe to enforce their dictates upon the people. That cannot be denied. Over time, the consequences for resistance escalated to a level of persecution the world had never seen. This is also a historical fact. God asks His people to educate and not to criticize or condemn. We are to help others see the truth for their own sake. I do this out of love. My own grandmother was a staunch Catholic, and although I was not, I wrestled with some of the concepts you might now be fuming over. I could not imagine that there was anything amiss within the Catholic Church's doctrine. It took the Spirit of God to convict me of these facts, and I pray you will listen to that still, small voice which says, this is the truth.

Men such as William Tyndale, Martin Luther, Jerome and Hess, Albert Zwingli, and many others sowed the seeds of the reformation. With the help of the Holy Spirit, these brave men deciphered much of the prophecies of Daniel and Revelation. They understood the reality of Rome's atrocities, and their resulting protests against the Papal system became the namesake of the religion they founded: Protestantism. Most Catholics and Protestants do not know the history of their churches, and what we touch on in this writing does not even amount to a smattering of what occurred. Nevertheless, I do not want my readers' eyes to glaze over with an endless play by play of names, dates, and events. Instead, we wish to concentrate our efforts on the spiritual relevance of Rome's character and activities because this is the kingdom that will one day regain the fullness if its power.

Rome would not allow the reformers free reign to spread the truth of the gospel. So, they intensified persecution of the saints, suppressed the Bible, and contrived doctrines to change the interpretation of the prophetic timeline. Without the scriptures readily available for comparison, many people adopted one of these concepts, ensuring the anonymity of the little horn and masking his deeds in the eyes of the unlearned.

"And when he had opened the fifth seal, I saw under the altar the souls of them that were slain for the word of God, and for the testimony which they held: And they cried with a loud voice, saying, How long, O Lord, holy and true, dost thou not judge and avenge our blood on them that dwell on the earth?" (Rev. 6:9, 10).

Ironically, it was not a spiritual awakening in Europe that brought 1260 years of papal dominance to an end. In the late eighteenth century, the French people had grown weary of their monarchy and the Church of Rome, which they believed controlled them. The French Revolution ensued and ushered in a tragic era of social and spiritual anarchy. In 1793, a formal declaration of nationalized atheism and a government decree banning the Bible completed the downfall of French society. They had lowered themselves to the equivalent of Sodom and Egypt. A relentless and bloody persecution of Protestants began. Millions of innocent Christians lost their lives. Seeing the horrors wrought by renouncing the divine standard of morality, the same French legislature repealed that law just three and one-half years later.

The Papal system no longer reigned over the people in the manner it once did. In 1798, General Berthier marched into Rome under the command of Napoleon I and captured Pope Pius V1. Berthier sent him into exile, and the pope died the following year. The head of the church had received a deadly wound and would for a time not enjoy the power they had held for over twelve centuries. Revelation 11 presents us an amazing metaphorical depiction of this entire saga.

"These are the two olive trees, and the two candlesticks standing before the God of the earth. And if any man will hurt them, fire proceedeth out of their mouth, and devoureth their enemies: and if any man will hurt them, he must in this manner be killed. These have power to shut heaven, that it rain not in the days of their prophecy: and have power over waters to turn them to blood, and to smite the earth with all plagues, as often as they will. And when they shall have finished their testimony, the beast that ascendeth out of the bottomless pit shall make war against them, and shall overcome them, and kill them" (Rev. 11:4–7).

Futurists would have us believe the two witnesses are a pair of fire-breathing, Typhoid Mary's. Remaining true to our standard of scrutinizing historical precedents to establish an interpretation, no prophet on record ever demonstrated those characteristics. Ascribing such fantastic abilities to human beings is not only wild speculation, it is silly. Generally, when the Lord's messengers bore a testimony, the residents of the region frequently drove them out of town, had them thrown in prison, or simply killed them, often in horrible ways. That is how these two prophets appear to end up but not before they accomplish some truly amazing feats—that is, if they had actually been human. Could it be that the Bible is not referring to people or supernatural beings at all?

In order to understand who or what these two witnesses are, let us examine the first verse to describe them. The two olive trees and the two candlesticks are the key to wisdom here. This symbolism points us back to the book of Zechariah.

"And said unto me, What seest thou? And I said, I have looked, and behold a candlestick all of gold, with a bowl upon the top of it, and his seven lamps thereon, and seven pipes to the seven lamps, which are upon the top thereof: And two olive trees by it, one upon the right side of the bowl, and the other upon the left side thereof" (Zech. 4:2, 3).

Immediately the Bible presents us with the same images we saw in Revelation 11. This is no coincidence. The purpose of scripture is to help us understand the truth. This is not done by compartmentalizing a verse here and a verse there then attempting to build a theology around it. It is done by comparing scripture with scripture to learn what the Lord is really saying. In so doing we decipher the mysteries and depth of divine wisdom.

In Zechariah, we find lamps fed by the oil from two olive trees. Each element, the lamp and the oil, symbolize something spiritual. The oil fuels the lamp; the lamp gives off light. "Thy word is a lamp unto my feet, and a light unto my path" (Ps. 119:105). Without oil, the lamp is useless because it has no other means of generating light on its own. Zechariah 4 continues, "Then he answered and spake unto me, saying, This is the word of the LORD unto Zerubbabel, saying, Not by might, nor by power, but by my spirit, saith the LORD of hosts" (Zech. 4:6).

Light is more than the literal means to allow the eyes to function. The light of biblical truth, the Word of God, is the means to make men see spiritually. "Let your light so shine before men, that they may see your good works, and glorify your Father which is in heaven" (Matt. 5:16). The word, the Bible, is the light of truth, and the Spirit of God is the oil that fuels that lamp. With unwavering clarity, the Bible makes this interpretation. Read the verses again, prayerfully, if you are unsure. In spite of all that he heard, Thomas would not believe that Jesus resurrected until he could see and touch the Lord himself. Truly, it requires more than words to convince some of the truth, and it takes the power of God to make them accept it in their heart.

"And Jesus answered and said unto him, Blessed art thou, Simon Barjona: for flesh and blood hath not revealed it unto thee, but my Father which is in heaven" (Matt. 16:17).

"Jesus saith unto him, Thomas, because thou hast seen me, thou hast believed: blessed are they that have not seen, and yet have believed" (John 20:29).

The two witnesses of Revelation 11 are the two halves of the Bible, the Old and the New Testaments. Their testimony in sackcloth demonstrates the depressed conditions for spreading the gospel under the weight of papal decrees, which banned such activity. Their power to bring plagues and scorch their opponents was a matter of perspective at the time. The papal system kept the people from learning the truth. Still, this did not prevent the church from making the people think scripture sanctioned their dictates and punishments. Indeed, those who defied Rome often had their allegiance to God rewarded with a fiery execution. When plague struck, it was a simple matter to convince the ignorant that the judgments of God were upon them for defying the church. Thus, when the cup of their indignation had finally run over, the French tried to rid themselves of everything spiritual, God, Bible, and church.

> *Light is more than the literal means to allow the eyes to function. The light of biblical truth, the Word of God, is the means to make men see spiritually.*

"And they of the people and kindreds and tongues and nations shall see their dead bodies three days and an half, and shall not suffer their dead bodies to be put in graves. And they that dwell upon the earth shall rejoice over them, and make merry, and shall send gifts one to another; because these two prophets tormented them that dwelt on the earth. And after three days and an half the spirit of life from God entered into them, and they stood upon their feet; and great fear fell upon them which saw them" (Rev. 9:11).

But three and one-half years after that failed experiment, the two witnesses rose again to stand on their feet and went forth with a power from the Holy Spirit never seen before. Revelation 11 is the history of the gospel through the dark ages and the reformation. This passage brings us to the early nineteenth century, which was the point in history when the printed word finally began to reach the masses.

Why does any of this matter? If one believes the biblical account ended in the first century (preterists), it might not matter. If one thinks the symbolism and metaphors of prophecy find their only relevance thousands of years from now (futurists), it also will have little impact. However, the point is that these are the historical facts and to choose to ignore this profound evidence of scriptural accuracy is exactly what the little horn hoped to achieve! We should pray for all who disregard prophecy's clear involvement in our history and choose instead to favor the Jesuit interpretations.

Chapter 7
A Delegation of Power– How Satan Uses Men

They shall put you out of the synagogues: yea, the time cometh,
that whosoever killeth you will think that he doeth God service.
John 16:2

Visions of the future were not limited to the prophets. In fact, the longest, most dramatic prophecy of the entire Bible came to a pagan king! Although the king did not understand it, the manner in which God revealed this truth testifies to His power and wisdom.

The Lord gave dreams and visions of the future to both Daniel and Nebuchadnezzar, the king of Babylon. In the king's dream, the features of a great image symbolized historically significant nations that were to arise (see Dan. 2:36–40). A head and shoulders made of gold symbolized Babylon, the chest of silver was Medo-Persia, the bronze torso was Greece, and the legs of iron were pagan Rome. The feet and ten toes of the image represented what was to come after, a divided kingdom comprised of iron and clay—two substances that cannot bond.

"And whereas thou sawest the feet and toes, part of potters' clay, and part of iron, the kingdom shall be divided; but there shall be in it of the strength of the iron, forasmuch as thou sawest the iron mixed with miry clay. And as the toes of the feet were part of iron, and part of clay, so the kingdom shall be partly strong, and partly broken. And whereas thou sawest iron mixed with miry clay, they shall mingle themselves with the seed of men: but they shall not cleave one to another, even as iron is not mixed with clay" (Dan. 2:41–43).

This interesting symbolism depicts an environment of spiritual disharmony. The clay is malleable and yields to the hand of the Potter (see Isa. 64:8) while the iron does not. The context of the passage speaks of how the two distinct entities resulting in the aftermath of imperial Rome will never again be able to cooperate in a manner that will form a unified society. The two entities are church and state.

The power of the true church, its ability to share the gospel, is inherently limited when the state determines how the people conduct their religious activities. The transformation of pagan Rome into a theological state, papal Rome, and the overspreading of this untenable relationship between religion and government throughout Europe, led to the most heinous era of persecution in human history. Although God mercifully cut that time short, the Bible tells us this iron-clay affiliation persists even in the last days, We know this because the feet and toes of the image are the final state of the world at the coming of God's Kingdom.

> *The power of the true church, its ability to share the gospel, is inherently limited when the state determines how the people conduct their religious activities.*

"And in the days of these kings shall the God of heaven set up a kingdom, which shall never be destroyed: and the kingdom shall not be left to other people, but it shall break in pieces and consume all these kingdoms, and it shall stand for ever. Forasmuch as thou sawest that the stone was cut out of the mountain without hands, and that it brake in pieces the iron, the brass, the clay, the silver, and the gold; the great God hath made known to the king what shall come to pass hereafter: and the dream is certain, and the interpretation thereof sure" (Dan. 2:44, 45).

In Daniel 7, the prophet has visions of the same four kingdoms, this time represented as beasts rising from the sea. The first beast was a lion, the second was a bear, followed by a winged leopard, and finally, there came a ten-horned dragon-like creature. In order of their appearance on the world stage, these animals identified Babylon, succeeded by Medo–Persia, which fell to Greece, and finally, Rome. The Bible names the first three kingdoms explicitly in Daniel 2 and 8, and Rome is the only major empire to rise in the immediate aftermath of Greece. Lastly, Daniel sees ten horns upon the head of the fourth beast and from these horns rises the little horn that we already spoke about. This little horn is the tiny kingdom that comes up from pagan Rome. It is the one that speaks great words against the most High and persecutes the saints for a time and times and half a time, which equates to more than twelve centuries. There is only one kingdom whose history matches this prophecy, papal Rome.

In Revelation, John reaffirms the dreams and visions of Daniel with a few of his own. "And I stood upon the sand of the sea, and saw a beast rise up out of the sea, having seven heads and ten horns, and upon his horns ten crowns, and upon his heads the name of blasphemy. And the beast which I saw was like unto a leopard, and his feet were as the feet of a bear, and his mouth as the mouth of a lion: and the dragon gave him his power, and his seat, and great authority" (Rev. 13:1, 2).

In this last book of prophecy, we find a fascinating correlation with the Old Testament. The characteristics of all four of Daniel's beasts are rolled into one multi-headed creature. What is interesting here is the manner that John describes the vision. The Old Testament presented the beasts in the order they arose in history. John sees them in the reverse sequence. Daniel was looking forward through time while John was looking back, and it is important to note that all the beasts lie between the two.

The last part of verse 2 is of key importance, "and the dragon gave him his power, and his seat, and great authority." Here we see a transition of sorts, a delegation of power and leadership from the dragon to the seven-headed beast. Using our biblical precedent as the interpretive standard, the seven-headed creature also represents a kingdom. However, this particular image, due to its complex appearance, represents more than the sum of its parts. First, let us see who the dragon refers to, spiritually and historically.

"And there was war in heaven: Michael and his angels fought against the dragon; and the dragon fought and his angels, And prevailed not; neither was their place found any more in heaven. And the great dragon was cast out, that old serpent, called the Devil, and Satan, which deceiveth the whole world: he was cast out into the earth, and his angels were cast out with him" (Rev. 12:7–9).

Satan is always behind any effort to persecute God's people, but the enemy does not work out in the open. In the mind of the unbeliever, the devil's greatest ruse is the perception that he and his army of fallen angels do not exist. However, he maintains a cloak of anonymity by enlisting the help of willing human agents within the church. There are notable examples of this throughout the Bible.

"And there appeared a great wonder in heaven; a woman clothed with the sun, and the moon under her feet, and upon her head a crown of twelve stars: And she being with child cried, travailing in birth, and pained to be delivered. And there appeared another wonder in heaven; and behold a great red dragon, having seven heads and ten horns, and seven crowns upon his heads. And his tail drew the third part of the stars of heaven, and did cast them to the earth: and the dragon stood before the woman which was ready to be delivered, for to devour her child as soon as it was born. And she brought forth a man child, who was to rule all nations with a rod of iron: and her child was caught up unto God, and to his throne" (Rev. 12:1–5).

Satan wanted Jesus dead from the moment Christ was born (see Rev. 12:4). Toward that end, he used the Roman appointed tetrarch, Herod the Great. Although the attempt failed, a nefarious decree from the king resulted in the death of every child aged 2 and under in the sleepy town of Bethlehem. Throughout Christ's ministry the devil used the Pharisees and chief priests as antagonists of the truth, and ultimately, it was they who convinced the Romans to crucify Jesus. Other than the reluctance of Pontius Pilate, it took very little effort from the enemy to inspire the cruelty of Roman soldiers toward the Savior of man. Nevertheless, Satan's ultimate goal went unfulfilled. Christ was victorious. So, the devil set his sights on another target: those Jesus commissioned to carry the everlasting gospel to every nation, kindred, tongue, and people.

The Bible frequently uses a virtuous woman to depict a faithful people and a promiscuous woman to symbolize the wayward. Revelation 12:1 begins with an illustration of Israel as that virtuous woman who, through a difficult labor, gives birth to the Son of God. These are not the literal labor pains of Mary, but rather the tumultuous history of the Jewish people. The crown of twelve stars represents the twelve tribes of Israel, being clothed by the sun symbolizes the righteousness of Christ, and the moon under her feet is the covenant on which she stands.

Let us digress for a moment and explain an important concept here. First, notice that the woman has the moon under her feet. In other words, she is standing on it. This indicates a foundation. The moon generates no light of its own. Like a mirror, it can only reflect the light of the sun. This is the essence of the covenant between man and God. If we seek to acquire the divine nature and reflect the image and glory of God, the Sun of righteousness (see Mal. 4:2), Christ, will become our spiritual garment. By surrendering our will, the indwelling power of the Holy Spirit performs the miracle of conversion and reproduces the character of God in us. If we seek His face with our whole heart, He will give us divine power to overcome. If we have faith, God enables us to claim the righteousness of Christ.

It was Satan's intent to destroy the Son of God before the Lord entered into His ministry. The devil failed in that goal, and the cross brought home the reality of his situation—he had also lost the war. Nevertheless, the devil still remains our accuser. His pride and hostility toward Christ and humanity compels him to thwart the redemption of God's people. He continues the war out of spite. Thus, while Jesus, the object of Satan's hatred, is beyond the dragon's reach, the Lord's people are not.

"Be sober, be vigilant; because your adversary the devil, as a roaring lion, walketh about, seeking whom he may devour" (1 Peter 5:8).

As we said earlier, the virtuous woman mentioned at the start of Revelation 12 represents God's faithful people, the true church. The texts are a very broad encapsulation of history up to the beginning of the new covenant, when Christ ascended to begin His heavenly ministry. Read these next six verses carefully and prayerfully.

"And the woman fled into the wilderness, where she hath a place prepared of God, that they should feed her there a thousand two hundred and threescore days" (Rev. 12:6).

"And when the dragon saw that he was cast unto the earth, he persecuted the woman which brought forth the man child. And to the woman were given two wings of a great eagle, that she might fly into the wilderness, into her place, where she is nourished for a time, and times, and half a time, from the face of the serpent. And the serpent cast out of his mouth water as a flood after the woman, that he might cause her to be carried away of the flood. And the earth helped the woman, and the earth opened her mouth, and swallowed up the flood which the dragon cast out of his mouth. And the dragon was wroth with the woman, and went to make war with the remnant of her seed, which keep the commandments of God, and have the testimony of Jesus Christ" (Rev. 12:13-17).

By surrendering our will, the indwelling power of the Holy Spirit performs the miracle of conversion and reproduces the character of God in us.

The woman, God's faithful people, became the target of Satan's wrath. The survivors of persecution fled into the wilderness to escape the prospect of complete extermination. Verses 15 and 16 refer to a "flood" and how the devil tries to eliminate them. We have already stated that Satan uses willing accomplices among men to perform his dirty work. The waters of a flood are a metaphor for such an occasion.

"The sorrows of death compassed me, and the floods of ungodly men made me afraid" (Ps. 18:4).

Recall from Daniel 7:25 that the little horn, papal Rome, persecutes the saints for a duration given as a "time and times and the dividing of time." Notice now that the length of time the woman takes refuge in the wilderness is explained in two ways—"a thousand two hundred and threescore days" and "a time and times and half a time." These two passages refer to the same length of time. But more than that, they refer to the same period in history that we saw in Daniel. This is another prophetic link between the Old Testament and Revelation. The saints, the remnant of the woman's seed and those whom the dragon persecutes, are the ones who keep the commandments of God and have the testimony of Jesus Christ.

"Here is the patience of the saints: here are they that keep the commandments of God, and the faith of Jesus" (Rev. 14:12).

The dragon represents Satan as well as his human subordinates. In Christ's day Satan used the state of pagan Rome as it was urged on by an apostate religious body, the Pharisees and chief priests. To reiterate Revelation 13, the dragon, pagan Rome under the control of Satan, transfers power and authority to the seven-headed beast. The passage continues:

"And I saw one of his heads as it were wounded to death; and his deadly wound was healed: and all the world wondered after the beast. And they worshipped the dragon which gave power unto the beast: and they worshipped the beast, saying, Who is like unto the beast? who is able to make war with him" (Rev. 13:3, 4).

Much like Revelation 12 presents the saga of the faithful church, the first four verses of Revelation 13 are an encapsulation of the beast's history. He acquires power and authority from the dragon and then, at a later stage, receives a deadly head wound. However, this wound heals, and soon thereafter, the entire world worships both him and the dragon. Next, John sees what the beast is responsible for over the course of its existence.

"And there was given unto him a mouth speaking great things and blasphemies; and power was given unto him to continue forty and two months. And he opened his mouth in blasphemy against God, to blaspheme his name, and his tabernacle, and them that dwell in heaven. And it was given unto him to make war with the saints, and to overcome them: and power was given him over all kindreds, and tongues, and nations" (Rev. 13:5–7).

The beast spoke blasphemy, made war with the saints and overcame them, and he spent forty-two "months" doing it. Along with the biblical evidence, let us apply a little common sense. One thousand two hundred and sixty literal days is about three and one-half years. In Daniel 9:25 the angel said the prophecy would begin with the decree to rebuild Jerusalem and conclude after 2300 "days." That order went out from Artaxerxes I in 457 BC. Daniel also says from the time of that decree it would be a total of sixty-nine "weeks" until the anointing of the Messiah. Jesus was baptized in AD 27. If you exclude year zero because there is none, Christ began his ministry 483 years after King Artaxerxes gave that order. Obviously, there is something amiss in these numbers if we regard the timeframe as literal days.

"After the number of the days in which ye searched the land, even forty days, each day for a year, shall ye bear your iniquities" (Num. 14:34).

"And when thou hast accomplished them, lie again on thy right side, and thou shalt bear the iniquity of the house of Judah forty days: I have appointed thee each day for a year" (Ezek. 4:6).

The span of time given in Daniel 9 as symbolic days represents literal years. Sixty-nine weeks multiplied by seven days per week equals the 483 years that it took until Jesus entered his ministry.

However, a year in the Bible is somewhat different than we measure it today. The flood saga described in Genesis 7 and 8 tells us a biblical year is 360 days and thirty days per month. The passages under study in Revelation and in Daniel both describe the reigns of the beast and the little horn as the sum of three measures of "time." The singular of "time" equals one year. "Times," without a numerical qualifier means double that amount or seven hundred and twenty days, and "half a time" also referred to as the "dividing of time" is 180 days. The total number of these three measures is 1260 days. Now, using the biblical standard of 30 days per month, the timeframe of Revelation 13:5, forty-two months multiplied by thirty days also equals 1260 days!

The reformers understood the truth; the little horn and the first beast of Revelation 13 are the same entity, papal Rome. The seven-headed beast did not rule for a mere 1260 days. It held power for more than twelve centuries, from AD 538 to AD 1798 when its leadership finally received its deadly wound. Papal Rome no longer held the people captive to its whims or its theology. The system lost its ability to wield the sword of the state, and it was the state that inflicted the wound (see Rev. 13:10). But as John noted in Revelation 13:3 and 12, that wound was destined to heal.

Chapter 8
Back in Business–
The Healing of the Beast

*These have one mind, and shall give their
power and strength unto the beast.
Revelation 17:13*

Throughout history, the dragon reveals his character and intentions through the words and deeds of men. Satan's role in spiritual Babylon is unmistakable. On the other hand, the Papacy's role is a little more difficult to fathom. How could Rome still have anything to do with prophecy beyond 1798? Has the system not changed its ways? Did the reformation not play a pivotal role in moderating the mother church? What did John mean when he said the deadly wound was healed?

Whenever we seek to understand a biblical concept, we must consider the context of the message or warning. Papal Rome's downfall occurred within the milieu of her improper relationship to European rulers and tactics for maintaining power. Throughout the Dark Ages and the reformation, there was never a period when the Papacy enjoyed the favor of the people or shared any measure of the true gospel. When the atheistic French republic finally had enough of Romanism, their backlash was not an expression of hostility towards authentic Christianity. However, Rome's shenanigans did not divert attention away from Protestants who became the targets of persecution by anarchists and the Church of Rome alike.

The Papal system had long held sway over the people by insisting that the prosperity of the church was essential to their eternal destiny. They burdened the people with heavy taxes to support the very system that held them captive. The clergy offered plenary indulgences (absolution) in exchange for favors and services, in other words bribery, and encouraged false piety in useless acts of penance. Then there was the ultimate delusion in spiritual arm-twisting: the dreaded excommunication. This tactic duped the unwitting, including the highest in the aristocracy, to believe that getting kicked out of the club meant eternal damnation. Needless to say, scripture never sanctions such practices. In fact, the very concept of a priest claiming the power to grant a pardon for sin is exactly the blasphemy that the Pharisees used to condemn Christ. "Why doth this man thus speak blasphemies? who can forgive sins but God only" (Mark 2:7). The Pharisees mistake, though, was in whom they directed the accusation. They refused to acknowledge who Jesus really was—God in the flesh.

Martin Luther learned the reality of the gospel and of the Roman Church from scripture. Salvation did not hinge on one's adherence to the beck and call of Rome. Homage to the Papacy was not the basis of sanctification. Salvation would come by grace through faith alone in the Lord Jesus Christ. This was the truth that lit a fire in the very hearts of reformers. Unfortunately, this metaphysical fire led to the burning of saints in streets throughout the cities of Europe.

Today, there are efforts to mend the rift between Catholics and Protestants, but how does one heal a bond that historically never existed? Reconciliation is a profoundly Christian tenet, but Protestantism emerged for the very purpose of separating God's people from a system that held them captive by force and intimidation. While France dealt the Papacy a serious blow in 1798, the event did nothing to change the fundamental concepts behind Catholicism. Indeed, many new and troubling doctrines have since emerged.

"And I saw one of his heads as it were wounded to death; and his deadly wound was healed: and all the world wondered after the beast. And they worshipped the dragon which gave power unto the beast: and they worshipped the beast, saying, Who is like unto the beast? who is able to make war with him" (Rev. 13:3, 4).

The healing of the deadly wound has nothing to do with patching things up between estranged religions. Revelation 13 clearly expresses papal Rome's rehabilitation as a return to preeminence on a global scale. The Bible does not cast that development in a positive light. The image of the beast was not one of benevolence.

In recent decades, the Catholic hierarchy increasingly interjects in matters of public policy and admonishes state leaders on matters of social and political importance. Until the 1960's only one United States president had ever met with a pope. Since the Eisenhower administration, all but one has. Government leaders on both sides of the aisle knelt before the body of Pope John Paul II at his funeral. Most recently, in a country with a religious foundation once based on the tenets of the Protestant reformation, the same Roman Catholic cardinal delivered the closing benedictions for both major political party's conventions!

We see the spectacle every time the Pope travels abroad. The entire world is awed by the majesty of a papal mass and the stately grandeur of the priestly entourage. The senses lure thousands to the serenity and opulence of massive cathedrals, and people choose their religion based on the most pleasant surroundings. Many Protestant churches have adopted an architectural approach to evangelism. Absent the classical artwork and visual spectacle of a Sistine Chapel or St. Peter's Basilica, contemporary American churches leverage the appeal of modern music delivered over high tech sound systems accompanied by elaborate lighting and jumbo video screens. Though we may wish to convince ourselves otherwise, God does not want our worship inspired by what pleases the eyes and ears, and many express their choice of denomination based on those very criteria.

Today, even many non-Catholics regard the Holy See in a positive light. Notwithstanding the occasional poke at Protestantism and sexual foibles within the priesthood, many regard the public face of the Papacy as one of genuine Christian outreach and charity. The mother church frequently champions the battles over religious liberty and characterizes every legislative intrusion into freedom as an affront specifically targeting her beliefs.

If you look past the noble gestures and concern it often expresses for legitimate moral and ethical dilemmas, the doctrines and traditions of the Papacy still supplant many gospel truths, and they continually add to them. The reformers recognized the link between apostate religious dogma and coercion. Without the pugnacious character of the middle ages, it is difficult for many, even Protestants, to reconcile the role of the pontiff in prophecy beyond 1798. As we mentioned at the outset, the dilution of Christianity as a term, which once applied to those who accept the teachings of the gospel, now reveals itself in believers who regard the truth subjectively. How do we know? Because for most professed Christians, the differences in beliefs no longer matters.

The new philosophy of Christianity is that faith and doctrine operate independently of one another, and they simplify the discrepancies between Protestantism and Catholicism by rationalizing that they are only diverse methods of evangelism. Nothing could be further from the truth. Had Luther and others chosen to embrace the dictates of Romanism, they would have had no basis for reform! Rome persecuted to prevent the people from learning the truth because the truth gave them no control over men.

It is difficult for many to accept that the beast of Revelation 13 is the Papacy, and it is even harder to grasp that the system would one day reacquire its power to persecute. The Vatican is a tiny state, which could be the inspiration for the term "little" horn. It no longer has on-demand support from an emperor or king, and it certainly does not have a standing army ready to carry out its whims. Where do we get the inspiration and the audacity to declare the leadership of the largest church on earth and the smallest autonomous state, a member of the false godhead, a prime player in spiritual Babylon?

No one said the truth is easy. History simply bears out the testimony of scripture. The complete resuscitation of the beast manifests in a specific way—renewed hostility and means to oppress anyone who will not acknowledge or yield to papal primacy. In the final days, the beast focuses that anger on only a remnant of those truly faithful to God. These will be the people who refuse to bend a knee to Roman authority, who keep the commandments, and who have the testimony of Jesus (see Rev. 14:12).

> *Rome persecuted to prevent the people from learning the truth because the truth gave them no control over men.*

The sovereignty of modern nations and the seemingly benign relationship of the Papacy to the rest of the religious world today makes all of this seem so implausible. How can the beast ever regain the leverage and influence it once had in an increasingly secularized society? Romanism was never a religion that allowed men to exercise free will in matters of faith. That is still the mindset of the system. When people defy the dictates of the Rome, they face retribution in some form. Yet Catholicism is not the only religion that has ever sought to control the population by force. That is why the Bible tells us she receives help from the third member of Spiritual Babylon.

Chapter 9
The False Prophet– Not Who You Might Expect

*Woe be unto the pastors that destroy and scatter
the sheep of my pasture! saith the Lord.
Jeremiah 23:1*

The conclusion of the previous chapter might have left the reader making some assumptions. The coercive nature of certain Islamic factions comes to mind. A detailed study of this religion takes us well beyond the bounds of this testimony. Though we might see many parallels in its behavior with end time themes, we must keep the character of the biblical false prophet in perspective. Islamists do not peddle any sort of gospel of Jesus. Although moderate factions claim to respect Christ, none professes a belief in Him as God or the Messiah. Muslims do not acknowledge that the Jews were the chosen people, and their hostility towards Israel still stems from a dispute over the birthrights of Isaac and Ishmael dating back to the days of Abraham. Islam may try to compel allegiance to their faith, but they present no spiritual complications to the doctrines or beliefs within Christianity.

Does this mean Islam plays no role in last day events? Spiritually speaking, they do not. However, many have seen first-hand how terrorism and violence toward Israel and the west have a way of shaping public policy and the tactics for dealing with it by both government and churches. Although Jihadists cast no particular spiritual impediments before the Christian, their activities have invoked everything from appeasement strategies by the state to protests by the churches. These may lead to restraints on speech and spirituality that we should all enjoy freely and instead propel the edicts that demand allegiance to the system, which will proclaim itself (not Jesus) as the only hope for humanity.

Though many Christians believe their salvation hinges on standing side by side with Israel to confront hostile elements, this concept is an example of the false teaching in their very midst. Jews are not the "Israel" of the New Testament. All too often we hear about Armageddon as the culmination of the ancient conflict in the Middle East, which in some theological camps spills over to the rest of the world, i.e. World War III in the conventional and/or nuclear sense. This is not what the Bible teaches. We will soon learn that the final conflict, Armageddon, is not relevant to our location because it happens everywhere. For now, what is important is why Armageddon occurs in the first place and what it means for those on the wrong side of the outcome.

We wish to point out that the secular media routinely airs dramatic depictions of end-times scenarios. They infuse these docudramas with substance from various non-religious sources, a few eloquent sounding theologians, and a smattering of biblical texts, which are usually taken out of context. Do not place any measure of trust in these presentations. While only small portions of them bear any relationship to present truth, the vast majority of the "information" they provide is speculative and, in most cases, decidedly unbiblical.

For example, one so-called "expert" stated that Jesus came to earth to become the King of the Jews in the most literal sense. She then made the following assertion, "He failed! He died!" This fundamental lack of understanding is exactly the same mistake made by the people of Christ's day, and it demonstrates either purposeful unbelief or a profound ignorance of scripture. As Christians, we cannot consider such a person an expert. If one does not understand, or worse, does not believe the Bible, they are in no way qualified to comment on prophecy. How can we place any trust in people to unravel the mysteries of Godliness or the plan of salvation if they do not understand history or comprehend the mission of Christ? Jesus came to earth to rescue humanity from the bondage of sin and thereby provide us with the means to reunite with God. To do this, He first established His church, a spiritual kingdom, which teaches the necessary doctrines of salvation to the entire world. In this work, He succeeded wonderfully!

Tainted primarily with a futurist mentality, these television productions allow for a broad range of assumption, and this provides the obligatory drama needed to attract and entertain a large audience. Unfortunately, their conjecture focuses the viewer's attention on temporal events, wars, natural disasters, pandemics, and the like, but it completely ignores the spiritual component that underlies all of Bible prophecy. It is interesting to note how secularists are willing to consider a biblical explanation of the future, but they will do so only if they brush aside the religious connotations. Furthermore, this mistake epitomizes the fact that last days events will deceive most people, unless someone first educates them in Bible truth.

To this point we have spoken much about doctrine and pointed out some of the key problems with human concepts versus the true gospel. There is more to come. Yet, I must stress a point of significance far greater than understanding the doctrines we discuss here. God laments the lack of knowledge among his people because it leads to error. Knowledge, though, is not the requisite for salvation. There are many who know a great deal of Bible truth, but they do not live in accordance with it.

"Not every one that saith unto me, Lord, Lord, shall enter into the kingdom of heaven; but he that doeth the will of my Father which is in heaven. Many will say to me in that day, Lord, Lord, have we not prophesied in thy name? and in thy name have cast out devils? and in thy name done many wonderful works? And then will I profess unto them, I never knew you: depart from me, ye that work iniquity" (Matt. 7:21–23).

Living under the umbrella of faulty beliefs, perhaps not even that many, is not the basis of God's warning to flee spiritual Babylon. If it was, God would judge them according to their knowledge instead of their character. He calls them "my people" because He knows their hearts, in spite of certain errors. But without the knowledge that comes through the study of scripture, God is keenly aware that many of His people will squander their chance at redemption when confronted by a final test of faith.

Not every person has the same understanding of the Bible. Not everyone knows the clear distinction between justification and sanctification. Not all have the same comprehension of the commandments or what atonement actually means. God's true people are those who live according to the spiritual light they have, those with the attitude and deportment of a true disciple of Jesus. Charity, compassion and self-sacrifice in the service of others, is the essence of Christ's influence here on earth. In this regard, there are many people of a genuine Christ-like heart; and without such a character, no amount of biblical knowledge will save them. Although repentance is still a requirement, this particular plea from God is more about escaping the deceptions that lead people away from sanctification and toward eternal loss. This includes many fine people within the Catholic faith and other denominations where they do not learn vital truths as they read from the Bible.

"And I beheld another beast coming up out of the earth; and he had two horns like a lamb, and he spake as a dragon" (Rev. 13:11).

We return now to prophecy. The text above describes a new player. Its placement within the narrative coincides with the time of papal captivity. Notice how this newest beast arises from the earth. Contrast this with previous kingdoms, which all arose from water. The earth indicates a sparsely inhabited area, whereas Revelation 17 showed us that water represents existing population centers.

Recall that the first beast of Revelation displays all the characteristics of each of the four beasts of Daniel 7. With the exception of its two lamblike horns, John gives us no other physical description for this new arrival. He does not identify it. This means it bore no resemblance to any of the creatures either Daniel or John had seen up to this point. This is a new nation, which does not rise in the midst of densely populated Europe or the Middle East.

The two horns resembling that of a lamb are particularly important. Horns in prophecy represent authority. Let me refresh the description of the first beast, and bring to the forefront of a key distinction between it and the newest member of our menagerie.

"And I stood upon the sand of the sea, and saw a beast rise up out of the sea, having seven heads and ten horns, and upon his horns ten crowns, and upon his heads the name of blasphemy" (Rev. 13:1).

Notice that crowns adorn the horns the first beast. These indicate powers that are kings or kingdoms. The two horns of our latest creature have no crowns. Although these represent separate powers, neither is a king and thus the nation is not a kingdom in the strictest sense of the word. The lamb-like description implies meekness, a power structure that is benevolent and peaceful. Throughout the Bible, the lamb represents Jesus. Therefore, we can assert that these two distinct authorities have a foundation in Christian tenets. Are we forming a picture of what this nation is yet?

Just as horns identified the leadership of nations in the Old Testament (see Dan. 8), the two horns identify the governance of this new nation. Only one nation on earth ever rose with a fundamental structure comprised of two distinct sets of powers, neither being a king, and each having a basis in the moral precepts of the Bible. The uncrowned horns represent the unique and purposeful schism in the leadership of this society: a state without a king and a church without a pope. There has been only one nation in earth's history to meet this description, the United States of America.

If one believes this interpretation is speculative, consider this historical fact: the nation that gave the Papacy its deadly wound and the first country to recognize the sovereignty of the United States was France, and the year of both events was 1798! Moreover, no other society in history has a foundation that separated the two horns of authority, government and religion. This is a concept one must evaluate on the strength of the evidence and allow conviction by the Holy Spirit, but there are no other possibilities. Unlike speculative interpretations, which attempt to determine what event will match prophecy in the future, the United States fulfills its role in accordance with the biblical pattern, as it happened.

However, a very large question remains, and for many, it looms as a deal-breaker for the entire concept. How could the United States speak like a dragon? Indeed, what does this metaphor actually mean? The Bible continues:

"And he exerciseth all the power of the first beast before him, and causeth the earth and them which dwell therein to worship the first beast, whose deadly wound was healed" (Rev. 13:12).

In the nineteenth century, at the urging of Protestant leaders, many American states passed statutes that enforced abstinence from work, and in some cases, mandatory church attendance. Surprisingly, fines or jail-time were not the limit of this tyranny. In its earliest enactment, Virginia decreed a death penalty after three offences! Overly zealous proponents of the laws resorted to spying on neighbors and vigilantism. A most ominous development, and little known to most people, came in 1888 when the country narrowly escaped the enactment of federal legislation for a national Sunday law. It was defeated in committee after a heated debate.

> *There has been only one nation in earth's history to meet this description, the United States of America.*

Later, the Blue Laws, which exist on the books in a surprising number of states to this day, allowed local governments to carry out enforcement of work abstinence on Sunday. Although that has largely abated due to cultural and economic pressures, many of these laws still remain, and some even call for their renewed application. Older members of my own church recall encounters with police officers tasked with ensuring Sunday rest.

Forcing religious dictates upon people epitomizes the character of the first beast. Rome never tolerated open rejection of her decrees. It was not long after the founding of the United States and even before France made her status as an official nation that new world Protestants looked to the state to enforce their religious prescriptions for society. It was for that very tyranny that many fled Europe in the first place.

Today, the United States finds itself in the midst of an ideological struggle. Threats to religious freedom appear more from militant secularists than from any theological source. Regardless of current circumstances, the Bible does not always give us details leading to the fulfillment of prophecy. The times do not occur according to the wisdom or desires of men; they occur by the will of God.

It is not for us to determine the events that might fulfill prophecy before they occur. When it happens, those who understand them will know. However, this does not mean the Bible gives us nothing to anticipate. It is by faith that we trust what the Lord says through scripture, and this is what it says next:

"And he doeth great wonders, so that he maketh fire come down from heaven on the earth in the sight of men, And deceiveth them that dwell on the earth by the means of those miracles which he had power to do in the sight of the beast; saying to them that dwell on the earth, that they should make an image to the beast, which had the wound by a sword, and did live" (Rev. 13:13, 14).

The activity of the second beast escalates from tyranny to outright deception. The performance of miracles and heavenly fire are counterfeits of Christ's and false evidence of the Holy Spirit respectively (see Acts 2). These manifestations capture the attention of millions and serve to reinforce error. Unaware that they are witnesses to satanic power, the deceivers convince the ignorant that God is with them. The first examples of such deception entered Christianity in its earliest years.

"But there was a certain man, called Simon, which beforetime in the same city used sorcery, and bewitched the people of Samaria, giving out that himself was some great one: To whom they all gave heed, from the least to the greatest, saying, This man is the great power of God. And to him they had regard, because that of long time he had bewitched them with sorceries" (Acts 8:9, 10).

As the Lord works through the believer, performing wonders of physical and spiritual healing, the devil may perform miracles on behalf of the false witness, making them appear legitimate and, more importantly, authoritative. The Lord limits what the enemy can get away with just as He did when the devil tempted Job. However, this does not mean the temptations are not severe enough to succeed in the overthrow of our understanding and our faith.

"And no marvel; for Satan himself is transformed into an angel of light. Therefore it is no great thing if his ministers also be transformed as the ministers of righteousness; whose end shall be according to their works" (2 Cor. 11:14, 15).

There is little reason for anyone to think it cannot happen today. The devil is more than willing to imitate an act of divine intervention when it serves his purpose. Satan offered Jesus the world if Christ would worship him. Some believe this proposal demonstrates Satan's lordship over the earth. Their logic is: how could the devil offer the world to Jesus if he does not rule it? The answer is simple; the devil lies!

"... He was a murderer from the beginning, and abode not in the truth, because there is no truth in him. When he speaketh a lie, he speaketh of his own: for he is a liar, and the father of it" (John 8:44).

Satan is powerful and influential, but he is not in control! The world would be a total ruin if the Lord allowed Satan free reign. God permits the devil to enact a measure of suffering to refine the character of His people, demonstrate to the contrast between good and evil, and of course, show people why they need Jesus. Satan succeeds because people allow him to gain a foothold in their lives. What can we do to prevent such a hostile takeover? Submit yourselves to God. "... Resist the devil, and he will flee from you" (James 4:7). Nevertheless, with phony works in hand and millions duped by his most irresistible trickery, the second beast takes his suggestion to the next level.

"And he had power to give life unto the image of the beast, that the image of the beast should both speak, and cause that as many as would not worship the image of the beast should be killed. And he causeth all, both small and great, rich and poor, free and bond, to receive a mark in their right hand, or in their foreheads" (Rev. 13:15, 16).

It is important to bear in mind the spiritual nature of the verses. The passage is not suggesting the animation of a multi-headed creature. The heads of the first beast represents seven kingdoms, all of which played or play a role in prophecy (see Rev. 17:10, 11). Although each of those kingdoms added something (paganism, spiritualism, idolatry, and persecution) to the characteristics of the whole, the head, which had the wound by a sword, and did live (see Rev. 13:14), is whose image we focus on here.

"And that no man might buy or sell, save he that had the mark, or the name of the beast, or the number of his name. Here is wisdom. Let him that hath understanding count the number of the beast: for it is the number of a man; and his number is six hundred threescore and six" (Rev. 13:17, 18).

The image, the mark, and the number of the beast are three different things, and it is often misinterpreted by the media. Making an image to the beast refers to the replication of that system in principle. In other words, the United States will fashion a system that mimics the characteristics of the first beast and pays homage to it. When the image has life, people will acknowledge its existence. When it speaks, people will listen to what it says. When it proclaims punishment for those who disobey the command to worship, the image will have the force of law behind it.

Chapter 10
Antichrist

Who opposeth and exalteth himself above all that is called God, or that is worshipped;
so that he as God sitteth in the temple of God, shewing himself that he is God.
2 Thessalonians 2:4

The image of the first beast was a system of coerced homage and mandatory allegiance to the papal throne. In the so-called Holy Roman Empire, the state carried out the dictates of the church. European history throughout during the dark ages and much of the reformation bears this truth out. Kings, queens, and emperors across the continent were held under the papal foot and did the church's bidding for fear of their own condemnation.

The truth is that the Bible says the United States will eventually form a system that bears some semblance to the system of the past. The fact that much of society appears to be at war with Christianity does not render this interpretation impotent. The social and political pendulum swings both ways and sometimes very suddenly. During the French revolution, atheism garnered an apparent victory over religion with a single legislative act. They took it all back three and one-half years later.

Today, the struggle between Christianity and militant secularists has reached a fever pitch. Increasing incursions into religious freedom by local, state, and federal governments are encouraging a more strident offensive by the other horn of American power, the church, to maintain its autonomy and influence. The pendulum is swinging back.

We introduced the antichrist early in our discussion, not to identify him specifically, but to explain the spiritual nature of his doctrine and character. As John pointed out, the title might apply to anyone who comes from within the discipleship of Christ yet seeks to exalt themselves with a doctrine that denies the truth about Jesus. However, the references in 2 Thessalonians 2:3 to that "man of sin" and the "son of perdition" are not a broad-brush application. They do refer to an individual, but not one person in all of history; it refers to a position of leadership that only one person at a time can maintain, and all the men that have held this position are given these titles. Since we already understand the nature of the antichrist, it remains to determine who the specific references were talking about. Revelation 13 gave us four attributes.

The mark of the beast is one of the most abused of all prophetic interpretations. It is also consistently confused with the beast's number. Many assume the mark identifies the beast himself, which is why it is so often misapplied. Let us see how the Bible wants us to understand this spiritual designation.

"And the Lord said unto him, Go through the midst of the city, through the midst of Jerusalem, and set a mark upon the foreheads of the men that sigh and that cry for all the abominations that be done in the midst thereof" (Ezek. 9:4).

In this particular instance, God commanded a mark be set upon the forehead of those individuals who were not taking part in the abominations in Israel. The mark identifies not its source, but rather its recipients. Keeping the speculation out of this interpretation, the mark has no biblical precedent as a tattoo, a national ID card, or a microchip implant. This is important because so many anticipate a temporal fulfillment of this prophecy with some sort of technological administration. None of those ideas bear the least relevance to spirituality. Although the image is a matter of enforcement and the mark is an indicator of one's allegiance to the image, one still cannot receive the mark unless they choose to. The image is a system of forced worship, but the mark indicates that one has made the choice to accept it. The problem is most will not know they have made that choice while others think they have no right to resist. The mark, received on the forehead denotes agreement, a frontal lobe decision to worship the image (see Deut. 11:18). Once the image has the force of law behind it, all those who agree to abide by its requirements have the mark spiritually.

The same mark received on the hand is also not literal. The hand represents one's actions. A person may not comprehend the ramifications of worshipping the image, but because it has human enforcement to back it up, they agree to receive the mark by virtue of their deeds. In summary, one group agrees to give their allegiance to the beast by bowing to him willingly, and the other yields because they fear the loss of their basic liberties, such as the right to buy and sell goods as mentioned in Revelation 13:17. It was no different during 1260 years of the little horn's rule.

The number of the beast is also misapplied by popular culture. Again, it serves the enemy's purpose to foster any deception that blinds men from the truth. Part of the confusion comes from the translation used by English version Bibles. John refers to the number of a man's "name." The Greek word from which we translate "name" more correctly means a man's title, such as president of the United States, chief executive officer, or even public notary. Obviously, the beast's title is something more significant than a family name. In addition, the Bible describes this title as a name that is blasphemous. This is crucial. Too many associate the name of the beast with a single person, typically a person of no spiritual consequence, such as Adolf Hitler, Saddam Hussein, and amazingly, Ronald Reagan. Blasphemy indicates a direct affront to the dominion or authority of God. Hitler and Hussein may have suffered from a god-complex, but neither tried to supplant the gospel with a theology of their own.

Recall the wounded head of the first beast represents the papal system, which does not just include the present man involved, but all the men who ever bore the Latin title Vicarivs Filii Dei. Vicar of Christ is the common English version of this name, and it still applies to the Bishop of Rome, the Pope. The wisdom John spoke about in verse 18 is the understanding that those words are a title given to many men. He also spoke of how its letters correspond to Roman numerals, VICIV–III–DI, which tabulate to six hundred sixty-six. This number, deciphered long ago, is from the inscription on the papal miter. The title "vicarivus" implies that the Papacy is the substitute for Christ on earth. This is not my opinion.

The following excerpts are from documents recorded over a span of hundreds of years, and they clearly demonstrate what Romanism believes and teaches about its leadership.

> We also define that the holy apostolic see and the Roman Pontiff hold the primacy over the whole world.[1]
>
> "All the names which are attributed to Christ in Scripture, implying His supremacy over the church, are also attributed to the Pope." Bellamin, "On the authority of Councils."[2]
>
> ... we promulgate anew the definition of the ecumenical Council of Florence, which must be believed by all faithful Christians, namely that the Apostolic See and the Roman Pontiff hold a world-wide primacy, and that the Roman Pontiff is the successor of blessed Peter, the prince of the apostles, true vicar of Christ, head of the whole Church and father and teacher of all Christian people.[3]
>
> The Pope is not only the representative of Jesus Christ, he is Jesus Christ himself, hidden under the veil of flesh. The Catholic National July 1895.[4]

Finally, compare the concepts in the following two paragraphs from the Second Vatican Council, which convened from 1962 to 1965. The document reasserts the concepts espoused 100 years earlier.

> The Head of this Body is Christ. He is the image of the invisible God and in Him all things came into being. He is before all creatures and in Him all things hold together. He is the head of the Body which is the Church. He is the beginning, the firstborn from the dead, that in all things he might hold the first place. By the greatness of His power He rules in heaven and the things on earth, and with his all-surpassing perfection and way of acting He fills the whole body with the riches of his glory.[5]
>
> This Sacred Council, following closely in the footsteps of the First Vatican Council, with that Council teaches and declares that Jesus Christ, the eternal Shepherd, established

---

[1] "Ecumenical Council of Florence (1438-1445)," Eternal Word Television Network: Global Catholic Network, http://pages.uoregon.edu/sshoemak/325/texts/florence.htm (accessed February 19, 2013).

[2] "EWTN Catholic Q&A," Eternal Word Television Network: Global Catholic Network, http://www.ewtn.com/vexperts/showmessage_print.asp?number=386119&language=en (accessed February 19, 2013).

[3] "First Vatican Council (1869–1870)," Eternal Word Television Network: Global Catholic Network, http://www.ewtn.com/library/councils/v1.htm#6 (accessed February 19, 2013).

[4] "EWTN Catholic Q&A," Eternal Word Television Network: Global Catholic Network, http://www.ewtn.com/vexperts/showmessage_print.asp?number=386119&language=en (accessed February 19, 2013).

[5] "LUMEN GENTIUM: Dogmatic Constitution on the Church, Second Vatican Council," Eternal Word Television Network: Global Catholic Network, http://www.ewtn.com/library/councils/v2church.htm (accessed February 19, 2013).

His holy Church, having sent forth the apostles as He Himself had been sent by the Father; and He willed that their successors, namely the bishops, should be shepherds in His Church even to the consummation of the world. And in order that the episcopate itself might be one and undivided, He placed Blessed Peter over the other apostles, and instituted in him a permanent and visible source and foundation of the unity of faith and communion. And all this teaching about the institution, the perpetuity, the meaning and reason for the sacred primacy of the Roman Pontiff and of his infallible magisterium, this Sacred Council again proposes to be firmly believed by all the faithful. Continuing in that same undertaking, this Council is resolved to declare and proclaim before all men the doctrine concerning bishops, the successors of the apostles, who together with the successor of Peter, the Vicar of Christ, the visible Head of the whole Church, govern the house of the living God.[6]

In the first paragraph, the document correctly asserts the dominion of Christ as indicated by scripture. However, in the second paragraph, the church ascribes the same power and authority to the pope! As we said earlier, the term "Vicar" of Christ means substitute or replacement. The early reformers, such as Martin Luther and others, recognized this usurpation of God's sovereignty. They understood the blasphemy of men who elevated themselves to the status of the Almighty by claiming the right and the power to judge the heart, condemn the sinner, and feign divine mercy with a grant of absolution, " … who can forgive sins but God only?" (Mark 2:7). Truly, these pronouncements of papal authority exceed even the Lord's! The Son lowered himself to become equal with man, but He never raised man to become equal with the Father!

"Who opposeth and exalteth himself above all that is called God, or that is worshipped; so that he as God sitteth in the temple of God, shewing himself that he is God" (2 Thess. 2:2–4)

I take no pleasure in the fact that scripture, history, and the declarations of Romanism itself proclaim the identity of the antichrist as the papacy. Truly, those dismayed and even angered by these facts have very likely been conditioned by preconceived notions. When I first encountered this concept in my own studies, I sought ways to disprove it. It was unfathomable that someone of a demeanor such as John Paul II could in any way be associated with these texts. Nevertheless, the description of the antichrist does not render for us one's personality; it describes his theological tilt.

The rationale behind the Roman ecclesiastical hierarchy comes largely through a misappropriation of Matthew 16:17–19 and John 20:21–23. From these texts the Church of Rome fashions the role of the popes as the apostolic successors to Peter. However, Christ does not refer to Peter as the foundation of the church. Translated from the Greek word, *petros*, Peter literally means a piece of rock or a rolling stone. The word Jesus used, which English Bibles translate as "rock," is *petra*. This refers to a large, immovable mass of stone. Christ was contrasting himself with Peter. He is the one doing the building, not Peter, and the Rock upon which Christ builds His church is Himself.

---

6   Ibid.

"And did all drink the same spiritual drink: for they drank of that spiritual Rock that followed them: and that Rock was Christ" (1 Cor. 10:4).

Satan used Peter to try to talk Jesus out of going to Jerusalem. Peter also succumbed to the enemy a second time when he denied the Lord three times. Despite his history, Peter ultimately became the quintessential evangelist, but no religion was ever founded on him. Jesus placed no man at the head of His church, and the only authority He gave His disciples was to teach.

Moreover, Matthew 16:19 says, "And I will give unto thee the keys of the kingdom of heaven: and whatsoever thou shalt bind on earth shall be bound in heaven: and whatsoever thou shalt loose on earth shall be loosed in heaven." This did not delegate to Peter or any man God's authority to forgive sins. The words of Christ, the sharing of the gospel are the keys to heaven. Christ alone is the way to salvation. A church can only joyfully and gratefully accept the sincere repentance of the sinner as a result of its ministry, and heaven records the conversion of that soul. But no man has the right or the power to absolve a person of their sins. That right belongs to God alone. Men who try to usurp that power are committing blasphemy.

"Thus saith the LORD; Cursed be the man that trusteth in man, and maketh flesh his arm, and whose heart departeth from the LORD" (Jer. 17:5).

Similarly, the second beast, fulfilling the role as the false prophet, is also not one individual. The overspreading of miracles and false evidence of the Holy Spirit manifest in many churches and those who profess Jesus with their lips, but reject him in their deeds, acknowledge these fraudulent signs as authentic works of divine power. Such churches lure unsuspecting congregants with promises of what God will do for them with no mention of what they must do for God. For example, we already mentioned the fallacy of "once save always saved," which some call cheap grace. This is the notion that faith requires no commitment beyond a verbal acknowledgement of Christ's sacrifice. They accept the Lord's death, but they reject the small burden of his yolk. To believe that God the Father, who paid the ransom for our redemption with the sacrifice of His own son, expects nothing from us epitomizes false teaching.

"I beseech you therefore, brethren, by the mercies of God, that ye present your bodies a living sacrifice, holy, acceptable unto God, which is your reasonable service. And be not conformed to this world: but be ye transformed by the renewing of your mind, that ye may prove what is that good, and acceptable, and perfect, will of God" (Rom. 12:1, 2).

Another popular teaching, the prosperity doctrine, preaches the fulfillment of any and all material desires. Based on passages such as Deuteronomy 8:18, where the Bible says that God provides men with the ability to gain wealth, the concept emphasizes that all we must do is believe God has already given us that new car or that better job, and we will have it! The doctrine also leverages Mal. 3:10: "Bring ye all the tithes into the storehouse, that there may be meat in mine house, and prove me now herewith, saith the LORD of hosts, if I will not open you the windows of heaven, and pour you out a blessing, that there shall not be room enough to receive it."

Wealth used for the glory of God is not an evil thing. But what could divert a person's attention away from Christ more than a gospel that focuses on obtaining it? What degrades the purpose of faithfully paying tithes more than treating it like a 401K? There is nothing in these texts to insinuate that God will guarantee us material wealth or that obtaining goods is the reason for tithing! Blessings come in many forms. It was Satan who promised Jesus the world if the Lord would worship him (see Luke 4:6, 7)! These churches teach a version of the gospel that does not edify one to become a member of the body of Christ. They do not explain the need for repentance, self-sacrifice, or the urgency of sharing the truth with others. They teach a version of the gospel, which appeals to the wants and desires of their congregations. All such churches harbor the elements of false prophecy.

In Revelation 17, an angel bearing one of the seven last plagues gives John a detailed explanation of what he saw and wrote about in Revelation 13. "And upon her forehead was a name written, MYSTERY, BABYLON THE GREAT, THE MOTHER OF HARLOTS AND ABOMINATIONS OF THE EARTH" (Rev. 17:5). Describing Babylon the Great as a licentious woman, we also see she is a "mother." She has offspring, and the Bible classifies these children as harlots. In other words, they have her odious trait of spiritual promiscuity or fornication with kings. Recall that prophecy uses a woman of virtue in Revelation 12 to represent God's faithful people, his true church. Quite appropriately, the woman of opposite character symbolizes an apostate church. These offspring, harlots, symbolic for wayward churches, are obviously of the same spiritual lineage as their mother.

To answer the question of whom or what comprise the offspring of this system—it is those churches, which have inherited many of their mother's tendencies. These are any of the faiths that consider themselves reformed but do not practice the gospel they profess. These are the false prophets, the apostate churches of American Protestantism.

Most people will find this revelation (no pun intended) very hard to believe because they see no correlation between their brand of faith and Catholicism. This only demonstrates the urgency of the plea—"Come out of her my people." We have already noted the confusion that arises from the disparity of doctrines throughout Christianity. The Protestant and Evangelical churches are rife with manmade concepts. This is a hallmark of religious traditions inherited from the Mother Church. The doctrines of her offspring might not be exactly the same, but if men have tainted them with their own unbiblical and heretical ideas, they are no less troubling and no less dangerous to their subscribers.

Finally, we have the identification of all three members of spiritual Babylon: The Roman Catholic Papacy, apostate Protestantism, and Satan himself—respectively, mother, daughters, and the spirit of evil, a counterfeit of the godhead or trinity as some call it. The first member blasphemously usurps the place of God on earth and thinks to change divine laws and the prophetic timeline. The next preaches false gospels such as guaranteed and universal salvation, genealogical predestination, salvation by works, and a myriad of beliefs that harbor elements of spiritualism. Finally, the dragon helps them by performing miracles that will deceive the whole world.

"For such are false apostles, deceitful workers, transforming themselves into the apostles of Christ. And no marvel; for Satan himself is transformed into an angel of light. Therefore it is no great thing if his ministers also be transformed as the ministers of righteousness; whose end shall be according to their works" (2 Cor. 11:13–15).

Satan, the leviathan of the Old Testament, is neither a pushover nor is he stupid. He is cunning, intelligent, and more powerful than we can imagine. We cannot stand toe-to-toe with him and expect victory in our own strength. Many members of spiritual Babylon, who believe they are prepared to withstand satanic deceptions, do not realize he has already fooled them. The doctrines of his inspiration have set the stage for errors on the grandest scale in human history, and the unwitting will drive the formation of the image of the first beast to which millions will bend a knee in fatal submission.

Chapter 11
The Enduring Fable— Ye Shall Not Surely Die

For the living know that they shall die: but the dead know not any thing, neither have they any more a reward; for the memory of them is forgotten.
Ecclesiastes 9:5

Contemporary Christianity, much like the Jews, has a hard time accepting certain truths. To placate personal wants and fears, spiritual Babylon proposes many concepts that steer people to the wrong path. We cannot explore every aberrant idea, but Revelation speaks precisely to a time when everyone must choose to escape this system or perish. As conviction comes to the heart and one realizes that their spiritual life is bound to falsehood and lies, it is the time to escape. The question then becomes how to escape and where we need to go when the time comes.

Although that deadline still looms, there is danger in vacillation. Once the entire world has the evidence before them and the choice is clear, the door of opportunity will not remain open for long. The first 490 years of the 2300 "day" prophecy in Daniel 9:24–27 were set apart for the Jews to clean up their act. When John the Baptist anointed the Most Holy, Jesus the Messiah, in AD 27, the prophecy was in its final seven years. With Christ's crucifixion, the door of opportunity narrowed to just three and one-half years. The stoning of Stephen in the Book of Acts heralded the end of the grace period for the Jews as a nation. Temporal Israel could no longer use the old covenant as a doorway to redemption. Christ was now the way to salvation for everyone.

We do not have the luxury of waiting until Jesus appears in the clouds of heaven before we decide that the Bible is right. Our lives must have a record of faith. The patience of God provides all men with an opportunity to know the truth, but that long-suffering will end at the time of His choosing—when He determines that the gospel has gone to the entire world, it will mean God's people have completed their work and those who will repent have done so.

"The Lord is not slack concerning his promise, as some men count slackness; but is longsuffering to us-ward, not willing that any should perish, but that all should come to repentance" (2 Peter 3:9).

Though He does not want anyone to perish, were it simply a matter of preventing it, the Lord would not wait for men to choose. God will not compel the conscience. He loves us, but our faith is the proof that we love Him. Furthermore, the Lord cannot relent on the death of the wicked. Their eternal destiny is also a matter of free will.

"He that is unjust, let him be unjust still: and he which is filthy, let him be filthy still: and he that is righteous, let him be righteous still: and he that is holy, let him be holy still. And, behold, I come quickly; and my reward is with me, to give every man according as his work shall be" (Rev. 22:11, 12).

The courts of heaven are nearing the end of adjudication. Each and every human being will have his or her case decided before Jesus returns. There comes a time, before Jesus returns, that the door of opportunity closes, and no one can change their destiny. The same concept is enshrined in the story of the ten virgins, five of which were wise and five who were unprepared for the arrival of the groom. When Jesus sheds the apparel of the priesthood and puts on the garments of vengeance, there can be no further atonement for sinners. Our characters must reflect the divine nature before that day arrives.

Revelation draws our attention to two snares: the deceptions wrought by satanic miracles and false worship. It is on these fronts that the enemy will attempt the final overthrow of God's true people. In Matthew 24, Jesus provided an extensive dissertation on end-time events. He warned about signs and wonders—that they would deceive the very elect (see Matt. 24:24). With this in mind, let us tackle the first problem, spiritual deceptions, because the Bible says these ultimately influence the masses to accept the dictates of spiritual Babylon and receive the mark of the beast.

"And he doeth great wonders, so that he maketh fire come down from heaven on the earth in the sight of men, And deceiveth them that dwell on the earth by the means of those miracles which he had power to do in the sight of the beast; saying to them that dwell on the earth, that they should make an image to the beast, which had the wound by a sword, and did live" (Rev. 13:13, 14).

"And the beast was taken, and with him the false prophet that wrought miracles before him, with which he deceived them that had received the mark of the beast, and them that worshipped his image. These both were cast alive into a lake of fire burning with brimstone" (Rev. 19:20).

Jesus performed more miracles of healing than He preached sermons. This demonstrated not only His power, but his preference for personal ministry over group lecture. It is certain, though, that without those signs and wonders, Christ's divinity would have met with wider skepticism. Similarly, His apostles expanded the early church by hearts drawn in through many of the same works. Amazingly though, the enemies of Christ often attributed his power to the work of the devil, a claim that Jesus refuted with unassailable logic.

"And Jesus knew their thoughts, and said unto them, Every kingdom divided against itself is brought to desolation; and every city or house divided against itself shall not stand: And if Satan cast out Satan, he is divided against himself; how shall then his kingdom stand? And if I by Beelzebub cast out devils, by whom do your children cast them out? therefore they shall be your judges. But if I cast out devils by the Spirit of God, then the kingdom of God is come unto you" (Matt. 12:25–28).

Inarguably, one of Christ's most impressive miracles was resurrecting a man who had been dead for four days. While eyewitnesses to that resurrection might have become instant followers, blessed are those who believe on faith alone. Today, it is deceptions about the state of the dead that cause the broadest swaths of Christianity to fashion doctrines that do not harmonize with scripture. Unfortunately, this causes millions to follow a path that cannot lead to salvation.

The miracles spiritual Babylon uses to deceive the world are rooted in the first lie the devil ever told man—Ye shall not surely die. Eve wanted to believe it, and in our age there are many who still do. It was always the Lord's intention that men have eternal life. God is a social being, and as any father loves his children, He created man for His pleasure, to love them and commune with them. Mortality was not part of the original plan, but it became the reality with the advent of sin. Had Adam and Eve passed the test of obedience and not eaten the forbidden fruit, they and their children would have enjoyed God's company and access to the tree of life forever. Instead, the death sentence for sin passed to all humanity, but Satan's great lie lived on.

The doctrine of an immortal soul makes the intimation that everyone is destined for some sort of permanent afterlife. Many of those who harbor the idea that our thoughts persist after death believe our disembodied spirits will go immediately to heaven or receive eternal punishment in hell. If that were the case, what is the point of resurrection?

"O that thou wouldest hide me in the grave, that thou wouldest keep me secret, until thy wrath be past, that thou wouldest appoint me a set time, and remember me! If a man die, shall he live again? all the days of my appointed time will I wait, till my change come" (Job 14:13, 14).

"Put not your trust in princes, nor in the son of man, in whom there is no help. His breath goeth forth, he returneth to his earth; in that very day his thoughts perish" (Ps. 146:3, 4).

"For the living know that they shall die: but the dead know not any thing, neither have they any more a reward; for the memory of them is forgotten" (Eccles. 9:5).

The King James Version of the book of Genesis does not say God gave man a soul; it says man became a living soul (see Gen. 2:7). This is a profound difference. Since the time of the Bible's oldest writing, the book of Job, the Bible conveys that death means the end of all living processes, including our thoughts. King Solomon, reputed as the wisest man who ever lived, reinforced the same concept. But even Job knew that a change awaited the dead. His hope was that God would remember us after our time in the grave. Despite this desire, he also made the unequivocal statement that the dead will not live again until that time when God calls them up from the tomb. The Bible says this in 1 Thessalonians 4:16.

"For the Lord himself shall descend from heaven with a shout, with the voice of the archangel, and with the trump of God: and the dead in Christ shall rise first."

With one exception (Moses), the dead receive nothing and go nowhere except the grave prior to their resurrection. The Bible says this event occurs in two stages: first for the righteous and a millennia later for the wicked. Moreover, as in the case of Enoch and Elijah, a special class of believers will never face death. These are the fortunate faithful who are alive to witness the second coming, the 144,000.

"Behold, all souls are mine; as the soul of the father, so also the soul of the son is mine: the soul that sinneth, it shall die" (Ezek. 18:4).

"The soul that sinneth, it shall die. The son shall not bear the iniquity of the father, neither shall the father bear the iniquity of the son: the righteousness of the righteous shall be upon him, and the wickedness of the wicked shall be upon him" (Ezek. 18:20).

"And fear not them which kill the body, but are not able to kill the soul: but rather fear him which is able to destroy both soul and body in hell" (Matt. 10:28).

The Bible says that the soul that sins will die. The obvious implication is that the soul that repents will live. In the context of the gospel, where God reserves eternal life only for those who are faithful, it makes perfect sense. The wicked and unrepentant will not receive that reward. The "hell" referred to in Matthew 10:28 is the English translation of a Greek word that means nothing more than the place of the dead, the grave.

The fact is that the Bible says we have no indestructible or everlasting consciousness. The word "soul" used throughout scripture refers simply to a living being; it is not some unique or perpetual manifestation of the human mind. We have no inherent immortality in any sense of the word, and God will certainly not grant it for the purpose of punishment.

The Lord takes no pleasure in the death of the wicked (see Ezek. 33:11). Why would He find gratification in their suffering? There will be no eternal life for the lost. Men concocted this doctrine of hell to scare people into church, but the teaching works equally well in driving them away.

Torture is not the destiny of those who reject God. The Bible refers to the final destruction of the wicked as the "second death." They will not only die, they will cease to exist—forever. After a brief resurrection, they will face the final verdict for their life's record and their loss of heaven will become permanent. They will perish with no further hope of redemption. Yet, compared with the imagination of men, the love and mercy of God prevails even in this strange act! The Lord knows if one cannot embrace the requirements of a holy life on earth, they would find no contentment in heaven.

Does the concept of eternal punishment provide a more forceful incentive to go to church? For some people it certainly will, but it fosters the wrong motivation. I once overheard a grocery store clerk talk about his pending baptism. He explained that he did not want to "burn forever" and believed baptism was sufficient to prevent it. This is a sad and serious deception to which many have fallen victim. We cannot base our relationship to God on self-preservation, the hope of escaping hell by engaging in a ritual. This misunderstanding of baptism is one of the many mistakes among the churches of spiritual Babylon.

> *Torture is not the destiny of those who reject God.*

Our justification relies on the merits of Christ alone, but our salvation hinges on faith in Jesus, a faith that we too must demonstrate by works of repentance. If this was not the case, why would we have to do anything? Though baptism is an important public profession of an inward conversion, it is not the end of our Christian walk; it is the start.

"But we are bound to give thanks alway to God for you, brethren beloved of the Lord, because God hath from the beginning chosen you to salvation through sanctification of the Spirit and belief of the truth" (2 Thess. 2:13).

Sanctification is the process of change that occurs as we surrender our lives daily to the will of

God. Each time we abandon our way in favor of God's way, we have allowed His Spirit to take control. Though we can never hope to match the righteousness of Christ, it is a goal we should strive for because it is the proof that Jesus lives in our hearts.

What about the biblical references to "everlasting burnings" or the "fire that never shall be quenched"? Do they not imply that hell is a place of perpetual torment? We answer that question with an emphatic, no! The texts refer to the fire itself. The verses do not say that anyone will burn forever. If one believes this is case of splitting hairs, please examine the following texts.

"For, behold, the day cometh, that shall burn as an oven; and all the proud, yea, and all that do wickedly, shall be stubble: and the day that cometh shall burn them up, saith the LORD of hosts, that it shall leave them neither root nor branch.... And ye shall tread down the wicked; for they shall be ashes under the soles of your feet in the day that I shall do this, saith the LORD of hosts" (Mal. 4:1, 3).

"Whose fan is in his hand, and he will throughly purge his floor, and gather his wheat into the garner; but he will burn up the chaff with unquenchable fire" (Matt. 3:12).

"Whose fan is in his hand, and he will throughly purge his floor, and will gather the wheat into his garner; but the chaff he will burn with fire unquenchable" (Luke 3:17).

In Malachi 4:1 and 3, the references to the destruction of the wicked by fire and their woeful destiny as ashes under the feet of the righteous harbor no ambiguity. The verses from Matthew and Luke refer to wheat and chaff, which are symbolic of the righteous and the wicked respectively. The chaff burns when thrown into the fire, but it certainly cannot burn forever.

"Then shall he say also unto them on the left hand, Depart from me, ye cursed, into everlasting fire, prepared for the devil and his angels" (Matt. 25:41).

"I am he that liveth, and was dead; and, behold, I am alive for evermore, Amen; and have the keys of hell and of death" (Rev. 1:18).

"And the devil that deceived them was cast into the lake of fire and brimstone, where the beast and the false prophet are, and shall be tormented day and night for ever and ever" (Rev. 20:10).

Many believe that Satan has literal dominion over hell and that he administers punishment for sinners. Of all the religious concepts, which atheists consider fairy tales, this one actually qualifies. When Jesus said hell was prepared for the devil and his angels, He did not mean for them to reign over. In Revelation, we see that Christ holds the keys to both death and hell, and Satan is the one who winds up in the lake of fire. If Satan were in charge of hell, why is he the only one to experience this punishment? As we said much earlier, hell is simply the place of the dead, the grave. In Revelation 20:14, we see that God ultimately destroys both death and the grave!

"And death and hell were cast into the lake of fire. This is the second death" (Rev. 20:14).

"And God shall wipe away all tears from their eyes; and there shall be no more death, neither sorrow, nor crying, neither shall there be any more pain: for the former things are passed away" (Rev. 21:4).

Finally, let us understand why the Bible refers to a fire that is everlasting and unquenchable. It is strange that people prefer to believe that hell is a place of eternal anguish and suffering. Truly and sadly, the vindictive side of human nature wants to see the wicked punished in this way. But that is not the character of God and it should not be ours, even in our thoughts. God does not want to destroy sinners. He wants to eliminate sin.

"And Nadab and Abihu, the sons of Aaron, took either of them his censer, and put fire therein, and put incense thereon, and offered strange fire before the LORD, which he commanded them not. And there went out fire from the LORD, and devoured them, and they died before the LORD" (Lev. 10:1, 2).

"Even as Sodom and Gomorrha, and the cities about them in like manner, giving themselves over to fornication, and going after strange flesh, are set forth for an example, suffering the vengeance of eternal fire" (Jude 1:7).

"Understand therefore this day, that the LORD thy God is he which goeth over before thee; as a consuming fire he shall destroy them, and he shall bring them down before thy face: so shalt thou drive them out, and destroy them quickly, as the LORD hath said unto thee" (Deut. 9:3).

"For our God is a consuming fire" (Heb. 12:29).

"And they went up on the breadth of the earth, and compassed the camp of the saints about, and the beloved city: and fire came down from God out of heaven, and devoured them" (Rev. 20:9).

"And the sight of the glory of the LORD was like devouring fire on the top of the mount in the eyes of the children of Israel" (Exod. 24:17).

God is eternal, which means the flaming tendrils of His everlasting glory are too. One day, He will rain fire from heaven, which will engulf the earth. It will endure only long enough to consume those who reject the truth. Just as Sodom and Gomorrah suffered the vengeance of eternal fire but no longer burn today (see Jude 1:17), the wicked will perish in the very presence of God. His consuming glory purges the planet of all evil and sin.

"And to you who are troubled rest with us, when the Lord Jesus shall be revealed from heaven with his mighty angels, In flaming fire taking vengeance on them that know not God, and that obey not the gospel of our Lord Jesus Christ: Who shall be punished with everlasting destruction from the presence of the Lord, and from the glory of his power" (2 Thess. 1:7–9).

"And then shall that Wicked be revealed, whom the Lord shall consume with the spirit of his mouth, and shall destroy with the brightness of his coming" (2 Thess. 2:8).

"But the day of the Lord will come as a thief in the night; in the which the heavens shall pass away with a great noise, and the elements shall melt with fervent heat, the earth also and the works that are therein shall be burned up. Seeing then that all these things shall be dissolved, what manner of persons ought ye to be in all holy conversation and godliness, Looking for and hasting unto the coming of the day of God, wherein the heavens being on fire shall be dissolved, and the elements shall melt with fervent heat? Nevertheless we, according to his promise, look for new heavens and a new earth, wherein dwelleth righteousness" (2 Peter 3:10–13).

God will not punish a man eternally for a short lifetime of sin. The end for those who reject God will be merciful when compared to the evil machinations of men. We must ask ourselves why we would look upon such a destiny with indifference. God is pleading with us to accept His gift of salvation because He longs to end the sin that ruins the lives of His cherished creations. It pains Him to see his children destroyed for a lack of knowledge. Every moment Satan seeks to further that darkness. Is not the promise of God worth the consideration? Jesus died so that no one need fear death. If we live for Christ today, we will live with God forever!

Chapter 12
Spiritualism– Miracle or Mass Deception?

And for this cause God shall send them strong delusion,
that they should believe a lie.
2 Thessalonians 2:11

Now that we have a better understanding of the biblical teaching regarding death, what a soul actually is, and the nature of hell, how do the errors taught by Babylon lead to deceptions that ensnare the whole world? What miracles will the beast, the false prophet, and the dragon perform?

We cannot predict every manifestation of demonic power. It is also not necessary. Whenever the enemy places a potential stumbling-block before us, we must subject it to the scrutiny of the Word. If any idea cannot measure up to the biblical standard, it is automatically suspect.

There are certain doctrines that piggyback on an incorrect understanding of death. Not everyone in the Bible grasped the concept as Job and Solomon did. King Saul, for example, sought the help of a witch to communicate with the deceased prophet, Samuel. The Bible does not say it was Samuel with whom the king spoke. 1 Samuel 28:14 says Saul perceived that it was Samuel, but perception is not always reality. If it was, there would be no such thing as a deception, and every doctrine conceived by men might be legitimate. The Lord makes the admonition against such excursions into the occult very clear.

"There shall not be found among you any one that maketh his son or his daughter to pass through the fire, or that useth divination, or an observer of times, or an enchanter, or a witch. Or a charmer, or a consulter with familiar spirits, or a wizard, or a necromancer. For all that do these things are an abomination unto the LORD: and because of these abominations the LORD thy God doth drive them out from before thee" (Deut. 18:10–12).

"A man also or woman that hath a familiar spirit, or that is a wizard, shall surely be put to death: they shall stone them with stones: their blood shall be upon them" (Lev. 20:27).

One might wonder, why does God command us to refrain from attempts to contact the dead if it were not possible? Popular culture encourages the idea that our dearly departed are walking amongst us and that communicating with a spirit world is both possible and desirable. Television plots abound with ghostly encounters and paranormal phenomenon. How ironic that so many in our society harbor a fascination with the supernatural when presented in the form of entertainment or pseudo-science, yet they reject it when the evidence points them to God. My friends, the Bible states clearly that the dead are in the grave awaiting (unwittingly) their resurrection either in glory at the coming of Christ or to shame if they have cherished evil in the sight of God.

On the other hand, Satan's army of fallen angels walk unseen in every quarter. This is why God's admonition is so important. The devil's minions listen to our conversations, observe our activities, and even watch what we eat. They record the details of a person's life, and once armed with this knowledge, they are fully capable of playing the role of any deceased person. By convincing people that it is possible to communicate with the dead, Satan gains a foothold in the unsuspecting person. They become vulnerable to his suggestions, and their thoughts are directed away from Christ. The devil knows exactly what your friends and relatives would say to establish your trust, so it is easy for him and his demons to act in character in order to achieve their goal. In fact, by entering into such encounters, deception is certain before the enemy ever utters a word. Once he has convinced you that you are talking to the dead, he controls you. The devil is a mastermind of deceit, and it becomes very difficult to sway the person under his thumb that he is manipulating them. God gave us the command to refrain from these activities, and He explains why.

"Regard not them that have familiar spirits, neither seek after wizards, to be defiled by them: I am the LORD your God" (Lev. 19:31).

"And the soul that turneth after such as have familiar spirits, and after wizards, to go a-whoring after them, I will even set my face against that soul, and will cut him off from among his people. Sanctify yourselves therefore, and be ye holy: for I am the LORD your God" (Lev. 20:6, 7).

We must place our trust solely in the Lord, His Word, and the prophets he has specifically chosen for us. By seeking the spiritual council of someone apart from God, such as a fortuneteller, palmist, spiritual medium, or even a horoscope, we subordinate our trust in the Lord to that of the adversary.

"So Saul died for his transgression which he committed against the LORD, even against the word of the LORD, which he kept not, and also for asking counsel of one that had a familiar spirit, to inquire of it; And inquired not of the LORD: therefore he slew him, and turned the kingdom unto David the son of Jesse" (1 Chron. 10:13, 14).

Endemic to the churches of modern Babylon are the doctrines of spiritualism. By confirming in the mind of worshippers that the dead can speak to us, the enemy implants concepts of heaven, hell, and an immediate afterlife, which are pleasant, but not biblical. This cements the allegiance of millions to false notions of salvation within their respective theologies. Offering prayers on behalf of the dead, seeking the blessings of patron saints, and most notably soliciting grace and mercy from Mary are beliefs steeped in spiritualism. There are no biblical foundations for any of these practices.

The wonders by which the beast, the false prophet, and the dragon hold people captive have already begun to manifest. Within Catholicism, there are ongoing efforts to formalize the church's stance on apparitions or ghost sightings, particularly those of Mary. It serves the enemy's purpose to make people think they have seen images of the mother of Jesus because she plays an important role in the faith of over one billion people. Nevertheless, Mary's highly favored status does not belie the fact that she plays no other part in the completion of the gospel. The virgin birth was the sign of the Messiah foretold by the prophet Isaiah. Beyond that, Mary's example of faith may deserve our admiration, but she cannot receive our prayers or supplications any more than you or I; she cannot bestow grace or intercede on behalf of the sinner because she was only mortal, and the Word ascribes her no other place in the plan of salvation.

Moreover, the basis of Mariology is similar to Gnosticism. To review, the Gnostics held the belief that Christ was sinless because He was spirit and did not come in an inherently sinful flesh and blood form. Catholicism holds a comparable view. The Church teaches that Christ's spotless life was due to a higher nature. They say that He had no part in the fallen human condition and that it was impossible for Jesus to yield to temptation. The Bible clearly disputes this (see Heb. 4:15). Had the potential for Christ to sin not existed, His victory would have been hollow and pointless. Though we can in no way explain the manifestation of God and man in one person, the Bible does tell us Jesus shared our burdens, felt our infirmities, and was tempted in every way that we are. His sinless life was not a forgone conclusion. Christ overcame by remaining obedient and steadfast in communication with his Father through prayer. Had he not done so, Christ might have stumbled and with him the hope of humanity. The victory He gained is the victory we must also have. His example must be ours.

"To him that overcometh will I grant to sit with me in my throne, even as I also overcame, and am set down with my Father in his throne" (Rev. 3:21).

The doctrines of Mariology assert that in order for us to reach Christ's level spiritually, we require another mediator, allegedly His own mother. Moreover, according to the church, Mary required a sort of prenatal vaccination from the stain of Adam's original sin into order to become the mother of God. Thus, they created a doctrine designed specifically for Mary, her immaculate conception.

These concepts are unique to Catholicism. The Bible never says Mary was sinless; it says she was "highly favored." In fact, Mary acknowledges her need of a Savior in Luke 1:47. We must also ask if Mary required a spiritually sanitized conception, why did her parents and her grandparents not require one as well? Where does that sort of logic end?

Additionally, the elaborate titles the Church of Rome gives Mary, such as co-redemptrix and mediatrix of all graces, attempt to elevate her role in the plan of salvation to one similar to and even level with Christ's! Therefore, on this basis, the veneration of Mary and reliance upon her intercession is a belief that opposes the very nature of Jesus and the redemptive ministry, which belongs exclusively to Him! It is a doctrine that is antichrist.

"Be it known unto you all, and to all the people of Israel, that by the name of Jesus Christ of Nazareth, whom ye crucified, whom God raised from the dead, even by him doth this man stand here before you whole.... Neither is there salvation in any other: for there is none other name under heaven given among men, whereby we must be saved" (Acts 4:10, 12).

One must wonder how and why Romanism would fashion a concept so clearly divergent from the truth. As we said earlier, Catholicism bases its tenets largely on tradition. How so many of these "traditions" found their way to the forefront religious dogma goes beyond the scope of this book. Many of them have roots in paganism. But equally, if not more disturbing, is the rationale the church uses for creating and holding on to them.

The Papacy teaches that the Catholic Church is the exclusive "bride of the Holy Spirit," and its priesthood is uniquely entitled to divine revelation. Amazingly though,

> *The veneration of Mary and reliance upon her intercession is a belief that opposes the very nature of Jesus.... It is a doctrine that is antichrist.*

the church came up with that concept on its own. Again, there is nothing in the Bible that states the Holy Spirit limits or restricts His council and teachings to anyone who sincerely seeks it. Speaking to all His apostles at the last supper, Jesus said this:

"But the Comforter, which is the Holy Ghost, whom the Father will send in my name, he shall teach you all things, and bring all things to your remembrance, whatsoever I have said unto you" (John 14:26).

In his first epistle to the church at Corinth, Paul made it clear that the only people who would not benefit from the teachings of the Holy Ghost were those who refused to listen.

"Now we have received, not the spirit of the world, but the spirit which is of God; that we might know the things that are freely given to us of God. Which things also we speak, not in the words which man's wisdom teacheth, but which the Holy Ghost teacheth; comparing spiritual things with spiritual. But the natural man receiveth not the things of the Spirit of God: for they are foolishness unto him: neither can he know them, because they are spiritually discerned" (1 Cor. 2:12–14).

God distributes wisdom and knowledge to anyone who seeks Him with an open heart. But everything taught by the Spirit comes with the sanction and support of scripture. If a concept has no biblical foundation, it did not come from God. Men have no right to claim that a doctrine is Christian simply because they find a way to link it to Jesus. Neither can a man claim spiritual infallibility. Incredibly though, this is exactly why the church maintains such an extensive and confusing list of non-biblical doctrines. Observe the following claim by the Church of Rome in this excerpt from the First Vatican Council on July 18, 1870.

> Therefore, faithfully adhering to the tradition received from the beginning of the Christian faith, to the glory of God our savior, for the exaltation of the Catholic religion and for the salvation of the Christian people, with the approval of the Sacred Council, we teach and define as a divinely revealed dogma that when the Roman Pontiff speaks EX CATHEDRA, that is, when, in the exercise of his office as shepherd and teacher of all Christians, in virtue of his supreme apostolic authority, he defines a doctrine concerning faith or morals to be held by the whole Church, he possesses, by the divine assistance promised to him in blessed Peter, that infallibility which the divine Redeemer willed his

Church to enjoy in defining doctrine concerning faith or morals. Therefore, such definitions of the Roman Pontiff are of themselves, and not by the consent of the Church, irreformable.

So then, should anyone, which God forbid, have the temerity to reject this definition of ours: let him be anathema.[1]

Imagine this: the Church states that the pope, whenever he speaks from the throne (Ex Cathedra) on matters of faith, cannot err! In other words, the Bishop of Rome, a man, is always right about religion because we say he is. Jesus never spoke or insinuated this idea. Once again, the church alleges divine revelation in arriving at this conclusion while simultaneously taking credit for the definition, a clear contradiction to the biblical concept of inspiration! Notice that the doctrine cites tradition, not scripture, to bolster their claim. This demonstrates the absence of spiritual light or understanding according to Isaiah 8:20: "To the law and the testimony, if they speak not according to this Word, it is because there is no light in them." The Bible explicitly mentions the use of "tradition" in place of God's teachings.

"But he answered and said unto them, Why do ye also transgress the commandment of God by your tradition?" (Matt. 15:3).

"And he said unto them, Full well ye reject the commandment of God, that ye may keep your own tradition.... Making the word of God of none effect through your tradition, which ye have delivered: and many such like things do ye" (Mark 7:9, 13).

The doctrine of Jesus Christ has no foundation in human traditions. It was not men who decided that Christ would die for our sins. It was not men who defined the meaning of justification. It is not by any human concept or rituals that we obtain sanctification. The Roman Catholic system has no more right to claim the title of "Bride" to Christ than any other church. Christ is wedded to His entire body of believers, not one sect. All those whose gowns are spotless and prepared to meet the Lord will enter into the joy of that celebration. No denomination may lay claim to an exclusive betrothal. In its own way, Catholicism would agree with this concept, but it would stipulate that their Church is the only legitimate manifestation of that body of believers.

The enemy knows performing false miracles will hold the hearts and minds of the deceived. Making people think they can see and talk to the dead is a key tactic. The papal system's endorsement of apparitions seals the deal in many minds and confirms their trust in a dogma that does not direct them to Christ. In churches without the doctrines of Mariology, there are still many concepts of the dead and an immediate afterlife that lead people astray. We already mentioned the error of praying for the dead. Apart from being a waste of time, it creates that false sense of security because it insinuates that someone can intercede for you after you are gone.

Mary sleeps like all whom the church ever granted a posthumous canonization. They await their

---

1 "First Vatican Council (1869-1870)," Eternal Word Television Network: Global Catholic Network, http://www.ewtn.com/library/councils/v1.htm#4 (accessed February 18, 2013).

resurrection, unwittingly, along with the every faithful person who formerly walked the face of the earth. But there is nothing anyone can do to change their destiny. If one denied the Lord in life, they are lost. However, all those now dead in Christ will rejoice at the sound of the Savior's voice on resurrection day.

"But I would not have you to be ignorant, brethren, concerning them which are asleep, that ye sorrow not, even as others which have no hope. For if we believe that Jesus died and rose again, even so them also which sleep in Jesus will God bring with him. For this we say unto you by the word of the Lord, that we which are alive and remain unto the coming of the Lord shall not prevent them which are asleep. For the Lord himself shall descend from heaven with a shout, with the voice of the archangel, and with the trump of God: and the dead in Christ shall rise first: Then we which are alive and remain shall be caught up together with them in the clouds, to meet the Lord in the air: and so shall we ever be with the Lord. Wherefore comfort one another with these words" (1 Thess. 4:13–18).

Chapter 13

The Times We Are In

*Saying with a loud voice, Fear God, and give glory to him;
for the hour of his judgment is come.
Revelation 14:7*

In the previous chapter, we explored the nature of deceptions that will cause many to pledge their allegiance to a system of false worship. In this chapter we will get a better understanding of the coming affair between church and the state, which instigates this event and the persecution of anyone who refuses to yield.

In order for the image to the first beast to exist and the second beast to enforce its worship, there must be a palpable construct behind it. The image cannot be merely philosophical. This leads us to the ultimate question: what will actually constitute enforcement?

Recall the biblical precedent set up by Nebuchadnezzar. The king commanded a public display of idol worship with a death penalty for noncompliance. It did not matter whether the hearts and minds of the people were in agreement with his mandate. It was likely no skin off the nose of a Babylonian or other pagan, and many Jews acquiesced to the law as a matter of survival. The king's proclamation included the means to force submission whether the people liked it or not.

This is emblematic of the warning in Revelation 13. There are those who agree in principle with the command to worship the image of the beast, and they willingly receive the mark in their forehead. Others submit by their actions and thus acquire the mark in their hand. With this in mind, it is extremely improbable that apostate Protestantism and government will collaborate to sculpt a model of the Babylonian/papal system with a ninety-foot statue of the pope. The paradigm is not the idol; it is compulsory homage to it, a concept which fundamentally opposes the character of God and the free-will He wants us to exercise in honoring Him.

Nevertheless, the Creator has never left it to man, and especially not his governments, to decide how best to worship Him. In Eden, the test of loyalty was a tree set in the midst of the garden. It was not a tree chosen by Adam and Eve. It may have looked like any other tree, but it was the one chosen by God. The first couple failed that test because they elected to believe Satan's lie instead of obeying the command of the Lord.

Abel worshipped by remembering the sacrifice God made to clothe Adam and Eve after the loss of their sinless spiritual veil. This symbolizes the covering man needs to survive the rigors of the fallen nature, the garment of Christ's righteousness. His offering was a forerunner of the Old Testament temple rituals, which pointed forward to Jesus. Cain, though, presumed to worship in a manner he thought should please God, the fruits of his own labor. When the Lord declined to respect his offering, Cain's response toward Abel became the first recorded act of religious persecution in all of history. The important lesson here is that true worship honors God in a manner He prescribes but will not force, and persecution of the truly faithful will always follow.

Historically, any kind of oppression is the product of man's attempt to control or exploit the lives of others. Using religion to further those ends clamps an extra set of fetters on the victims, ignorance. However, this does not preclude the possibility that an entire group may fall into apostasy willingly. In other words, a sect may become self-deceived. Unity among members of a religious denomination does not guarantee that their form of worship is in harmony with God. It is even likelier that a form of Christianity that does not espouse the truth will fall short of the unity that our Savior pleads us to have.

Earlier we asked how one escapes from spiritual Babylon. Revelation 13 explained what was going to happen and who instigates it. Moving now to Revelation 14, we find that the Bible draws a clear distinction between those who worship God, the Creator, and those who accept the mark of the beast. It is by understanding this difference that we realize what escape actually means.

"And I saw another angel fly in the midst of heaven, having the everlasting gospel to preach unto them that dwell on the earth, and to every nation, and kindred, and tongue, and people, Saying with a loud voice, Fear God, and give glory to him; for the hour of his judgment is come: and worship him that made heaven, and earth, and the sea, and the fountains of waters" (Rev. 14:6, 7).

Revelation 14:6 and 7, the first angel's message, is a global plea to revere and glorify God. Especially notable here is the announcement that judgment has commenced. For most Christians, that is a striking reality. How do we know this text does not portray events in the future? If the hour of His judgment has come, why are we still here? In the light of what we have discussed so far, these are fair questions. Most people assume the judgment is something that will conclude quickly, even in a single day. However, Daniel 7 confirms three times in separate passages that the judgment began in the immediate aftermath of the Little Horn era. Read the following verses carefully.

"A fiery stream issued and came forth from before him: thousand thousands ministered unto him, and ten thousand times ten thousand stood before him: the judgment was set, and the books were opened" (Dan. 7:10).

"I beheld, and the same horn made war with the saints, and prevailed against them; Until the Ancient of days came, and judgment was given to the saints of the most High; and the time came that the saints possessed the kingdom" (Dan. 7:21, 22).

"And he shall speak great words against the most High, and shall wear out the saints of the most High, and think to change times and laws: and they shall be given into his hand until a time and times and the dividing of time But the judgment shall sit, and they shall take away his dominion, to consume and to destroy it unto the end" (Dan. 7:25, 26).

The New Testament paints a picture of the same chronology. Recall that chapter 11 of Revelation details history of the Old and New Testaments, the two witnesses. Suppressed by the church and held in disdain by French society for the light it shed on their sins, the Word of God conducted its witness in sackcloth throughout the Dark Ages and reformation period. The decree to ban the Bible and the wounding of the papal system, the end of the little horn's reign, occurred at the climax of France's descent into spiritual and social chaos. Immediately after this age, the Bible gives us a description of events that match Daniel's vision.

"And the seventh angel sounded; and there were great voices in heaven, saying, The kingdoms of this world are become the kingdoms of our Lord, and of his Christ; and he shall reign for ever and ever.... And the nations were angry, and thy wrath is come, and the time of the dead, that they should be judged, and that thou shouldest give reward unto thy servants the prophets, and to the saints, and them that fear thy name, small and great; and shouldest destroy them which destroy the earth" (Rev. 11:15, 18).

The judgment mentioned in Revelation 11:18 refers only to the dead. Clearly, at this stage of history, the pages for the living were not yet under scrutiny. This demonstrates the nature of the judgment as a process that requires some measure of time. We do not know exactly how much time it will take.

The vision of Daniel and its explanation carry over to subsequent chapters. Continuing in chapter 8, Daniel hears that this prophecy concludes after a span of 2300 years (see Dan. 8:14), and he receives the starting point in Daniel 9:25.

"Then I heard one saint speaking, and another saint said unto that certain saint which spake, How long shall be the vision concerning the daily sacrifice, and the transgression of desolation, to give both the sanctuary and the host to be trodden under foot? And he said unto me, Unto two thousand and three hundred days; then shall the sanctuary be cleansed" (Dan. 8:13, 14).

The cleansing of the sanctuary points us to a ceremonial ordinance in the handwritten Law of Moses. The final act of the high priest's ministry was to purge the earthly temple of the sins accumulated from the congregation over the past year. This annual ritual was known as the Day of Atonement. In this particular passage of Daniel, though, the book refers to the final atonement accomplished by Christ, the true High Priest. We know this because 2300 years is well after the establishment of the new covenant. To understand the cleansing of the heavenly sanctuary, an explanation of the ritual in the Old Testament is essential.

For 1400 years the Jews rehearsed the plan of salvation. The earthly tabernacle and its services represented the entirety of the redemptive work Jesus was to perform. In front of their eyes, mostly blinded eyes, the people watched as the Lamb of God entered the outer court. When the Jews presented Jesus, the spotless offering to the high priest as a sacrifice, they did not realize what they were witnessing. Ignorant of the amazing prophecy unfolding before them, they watched the lamb slain upon the altar of the cross. None were aware that the doctrinal traditions, of which they were so proud and so jealous, had just become void.

Of all the symbolism in the Old Testament holy days, the Day of Atonement was the most important. It was a time to afflict ones soul for their sins and to pray for mercy. Though it was only conducted once each year by the high priest, the service conveyed the judgment of everyone's life record. Unlike the daily sacrifice, which allowed people to regularly cast their sins upon a sacrificial lamb, the Day of Atonement ritual represented the closure of the ministry within the temple, where those collected sins were finally purged. At its conclusion, the high priest emerged from the Most Holy Place and symbolically transferred all the sins of the people to the scapegoat, which was then ushered off to the wilderness by a strong man of the congregation. This final act represents the closing of Christ's heavenly ministry, the second coming, and the banishment of Satan for a thousand years.

"And I saw an angel come down from heaven, having the key of the bottomless pit and a great chain in his hand. And he laid hold on the dragon, that old serpent, which is the Devil, and Satan, and bound him a thousand years, And cast him into the bottomless pit, and shut him up, and set a seal upon him, that he should deceive the nations no more, till the thousand years should be fulfilled: and after that he must be loosed a little season" (Rev. 20:1–3).

When the Day of Atonement ceremony began, it was a new phase in the high priest's ministry, the start of judgment. While the priest was in the Most Holy Place making that final atonement, no man could enter the first room. This means the daily sacrifice, where a person's sins were routinely taken upon the lamb, was suspended. It was a probationary period, when the people could do nothing but wait, watch, and pray as the high priest pleaded the blood of the lamb on our behalf before the mercy seat, the very throne of God.

When Jesus Christ, both sacrificial Lamb and High Priest, ascended to heaven, He entered the heavenly sanctuary to begin His ministry in the first apartment. That portion of Christ's work was not indefinite. Like the earthly example, there would be a day when Christ would move His atonement work to the Most Holy Place, and the judgment would commence. This is what the scriptures explained for fourteen centuries, and they still convey to man two millennia later.

Recounting the fulfillment of Daniel's vision of the 2300 days, Jerusalem's reconstruction began in 457 BC. Daniel 9 provided the incredible waymarks of Christ's ministry—His anointing and, ultimately, His crucifixion. In chapter twelve, Daniel is still trying to understand the vision. The angel gives him another waymark, which includes the 1260 years of the little horn's rule that ended in 1798 with the exile of the pope. This leaves us with forty-six years to account for to reach the end of the prophecy, which is the year 1844.

In the span of those forty-six years (remember this is after the wounding of the beast and the "resurrection" of the two witnesses, the Old and New Testament's of the Bible), Christianity experienced a rapid global revival. The church blossomed. Whether coincidentally or providentially that was the same length of time the Bible said it took to rebuild the temple in John 2:20. Then, on October 22, 1844, it all seemingly came to a screeching halt.

Many believed that the cleansing of sanctuary in 1844 represented the second coming and the purging of the earth by fire. The date, though correctly deduced and calculated from prophecy, did not conclude with that event. The faithful who anticipated the arrival of the Savior in 1844 felt the sting of a great disappointment and the ridicule of family and peers who did not subscribe to their interpretation. Revelation 10 foretells of this saga.

"And I went unto the angel, and said unto him, Give me the little book. And he said unto me, Take it, and eat it up; and it shall make thy belly bitter, but it shall be in thy mouth sweet as honey. And I took the little book out of the angel's hand, and ate it up; and it was in my mouth sweet as honey: and as soon as I had eaten it, my belly was bitter. And he said unto me, Thou must prophesy again before many peoples, and nations, and tongues, and kings" (Rev.10:9–11).

The little book, sealed until the time of the end, is the book of Daniel. We know this because John's encounter with the angel bearing the book is nearly identical to Daniel's, and it occurs in the timeframe specified in Daniel 12, the time of the end. Daniel's book would be sealed from understanding and opened anew in the last days.

Gabriel told the prophet it would not be until the last days that man would understand the visions. The first post-little horn interpretation of Daniel made many think the return of Christ was imminent. Although they were mistaken, the sweetness of that prospect inspired a revival of the church with a level of brotherly love and dedication to the gospel not seen since the first century. Unfortunately, the excitement and anticipation turned to bitterness when Jesus did not come.

Undaunted by their detractors and inspired by visions and light from the Holy Spirit, those pioneers of the great Advent movement returned to their study of scripture, discovered their error, and set out to prophecy again. What was their error? It was a misinterpretation of the sanctuary message. It will be at the conclusion of the final act of atonement, mediation, and spiritual cleansing on behalf of the living that Christ will leave the sanctuary and return to earth. It is then that the devil, the scapegoat, will receive his compensation for the misery he has caused. My friends, we have been living in the judgment era for more than 160 years. It will finish in accordance with the words of Christ.

"But of that day and hour knoweth no man, no, not the angels of heaven, but my Father only" (Matt. 24:36).

"And this gospel of the kingdom shall be preached in all the world for a witness unto all nations; and then shall the end come" (Matt. 24:14).

Despite the clues in these verses, one must still wonder what is taking so long. Why are we still marooned on this sin-stricken planet? Are we truly waiting until the final vestige of humanity has completed a comprehensive Bible study? Is the world still suffering because the last boat to carry missionaries to some remote Amazonian village is stuck at the dock?

My friends, we are not waiting for God. He is waiting for us. He is waiting for a people who are prepared in the Spirit to enter the Promised Land. When the Jews left Egypt, their journey to Canaan should have lasted no more than forty days. But because of their unbelief, their disobedience, and their desire to hold onto the things of the world, God made them wander in the wilderness for forty years. Those trials and tribulations purged out the dross from among the pure in heart.

Revelation 13:14 nearly saw fulfillment in 1888 with legislation proposed by Senator Henry Blair.

The government came within a mere casting of votes from establishing the image to the beast. Jesus could have come many years ago, but His people were not ready; their hearts were not clean. Today, though there is still prophecy to unfold, only God knows how much longer it will be before He has a people worthy of their birthright, the heavenly Canaan.

"Saying with a loud voice, Fear God, and give glory to him; for the hour of his judgment is come: and worship him that made heaven, and earth, and the sea, and the fountains of waters" (Rev. 14:7).

We return now to our discussion of Revelation 14:7. The final phrase, "and worship him that made heaven, and earth, and the sea, and the fountains of waters," refers to the Creator. Many take this portion of the text for granted. They may profess to believe in Creation, but they simply assume God formed the world in six days, took the day off on the seventh, and that concluded the matter. But the passage points us back to a very important chapter of the Old Testament, Exodus 20:8–11: "Remember the sabbath day, to keep it holy. Six days shalt thou labour, and do all thy work: But the seventh day is the sabbath of the Lord thy God: in it thou shalt not do any work, thou, nor thy son, nor thy daughter, thy manservant, nor thy maidservant, nor thy cattle, nor thy stranger that is within thy gates: For in six days the LORD made heaven and earth, the sea, and all that in them is, and rested the seventh day: wherefore the LORD blessed the sabbath day, and hallowed it."

> *We are not waiting for God.*
> *He is waiting for us.*

Creation was no casual affair. That is why the world tries so hard to find a way around it. To acknowledge the incredible power and intellect of He who can speak the universe into existence is to acknowledge His authority and dominion. The so-called science, which attempts to thwart the Creation account, is not one of curiosity or an honest pursuit of answers. If it were, public schools systems would not ban Creation teaching.

Our goal here is not to argue pro or con for the subject matter in ninth grade biology or social studies. Although much of our emphasis has been on understanding the mark of the beast and how it signifies allegiance to an apostate system of worship, we must stress that there is a sign of loyalty to God, too. What has this to do with Creation? We were not there to see the formation of the earth. Science looks for ways to explain how it happened, but God knew men would never comprehend His ability to command the world into existence. Because of this, it was essential that man have the means to demonstrate acknowledgement of the Lord's power, dominion, and authority. A "thumbs up" to the concept of a Creator is not enough.

"Moreover also I gave them my sabbaths, to be a sign between me and them, that they might know that I am the LORD that sanctify them.… And hallow my sabbaths; and they shall be a sign between me and you, that ye may know that I am the LORD your God" (Ezek. 20:12, 20).

The passage from Revelation 14:7 is a direct quote from the fourth commandment. Why would the Bible not come right out and mention the Sabbath by name? Although the verse does not appear as cryptic as others, the passage does refer us back to the Old Testament so that we will take the time to study the matter thoroughly.

Where people believe that science promotes a viable explanation for the world's formation, it effectively mitigates or even eliminates the biblical account of Creation in those minds. Without Creation, there is no fall of man. Without the fall of man, there is no sin. Without sin, we have no need of a savior. Satan rejoices.

The wording in Revelation is no coincidence. The seventh-day remains our sign of allegiance to the Creator. Throughout history, the Sabbath was a chronic stumbling block. It still is today. Few people understand it as God intended. On repeated occasions, the Lord exhorted the Jews and any stranger among them to revere the day because they would receive a profound blessing by doing so.

"If thou turn away thy foot from the sabbath, from doing thy pleasure on my holy day; and call the sabbath a delight, the holy of the LORD, honourable; and shalt honour him, not doing thine own ways, nor finding thine own pleasure, nor speaking thine own words: Then shalt thou delight thyself in the LORD; and I will cause thee to ride upon the high places of the earth, and feed thee with the heritage of Jacob thy father: for the mouth of the LORD hath spoken it" (Isa. 58:13, 14).

The act of Creation is the basis for six days of work and a day of rest. The week is the only measure of time without representation in celestial cycles. The Sabbath is a special and unique blessing for the end of each week. It is God's desire that we put aside our personal pursuits for a single day and spend some time with Him. The command to reverence the seventh-day is not a constraint upon liberty as some perceive it. The Sabbath is a time to rest, fellowship, and rejoice in communion with God as we come apart from the cares of the world.

This is not a passive doctrine, one accepted by a mere nod of the head or pliable at the whims of men. The Sabbath is very special. Our acknowledgment of it through the observance God commands demonstrates our understanding of who God truly is. When we enter into that weekly rest, it does two things for us; it renews us, spiritually and physically, and it brings us closer to the Creator. Like any commandment, we do not keep the Sabbath holy to earn the favor of God. We do so because the Lord knows the blessing it provides and the faith it engenders.

Immediately after the first angel explains true worship in Revelation 14:6 and 7, a second angel proclaims the fallen condition of spiritual Babylon as a result of her many abominations. After this, a third angel delivers the dire consequences for worshippers of the image erected to honor the beast.

"And there followed another angel, saying, Babylon is fallen, is fallen, that great city, because she made all nations drink of the wine of the wrath of her fornication. And the third angel followed them, saying with a loud voice, If any man worship the beast and his image, and receive his mark in his forehead, or in his hand, The same shall drink of the wine of the wrath of God, which is poured out without mixture into the cup of his indignation; and he shall be tormented with fire and brimstone in the presence of the holy angels, and in the presence of the Lamb: And the smoke of their torment ascendeth up for ever and ever: and they have no rest day nor night, who worship the beast and his image, and whosoever receiveth the mark of his name. Here is the patience of the saints: here are they that keep the commandments of God, and the faith of Jesus" (Rev. 14:8–12).

In verse 7, the special emphasis on the dominion of the Creator indicated that the Sabbath plays a special role in distinguishing the saints, who keep the fourth commandment, from members of Babylon who wear the mark of the beast. Obviously, Babylon does not keep the commandments of God. But we also see a reiteration of the character first noted in Revelation 13, wrath and fornication.

Bear in mind that the mark of the beast does not exist until worship becomes a matter of enforcement, in other words, when it is the law of man. As the liaison between church and state seeks to compel spirituality, the image to the beast acquires its life and its voice through an act of legislation or decree. What could government do at the behest of the church, to ensure widespread compliance with a mandate to worship? More significantly, why would this occur in the first place?

"And because iniquity shall abound, the love of many shall wax cold. But he that shall endure unto the end, the same shall be saved" (Matt. 24:12, 13).

Throughout the New Testament warnings about the deteriorating state of humanity and the world are portents of the last days. As the world falls further into sin, the Spirit of God withdraws and the restraints placed upon Satan diminish. Natural disasters, earthquakes in diverse places, tsunamis, wars and rumors of war, disease, famines, and even financial chaos are all hallmarks of the end times (see Matthew 24; Mark 13; and Luke 21). Eventually, the planet reaches a point of degradation where society demands action. The churches will see our plight as the result of waning spirituality and unite to urge the government to intervene under the guise of the greater good.

I considered the benefit of providing examples of statements by prominent religious figures, Protestant and Catholic alike, who support a federal mandate for Sunday rest. Although these are people that every Christian would recognize, it is more important to allow the Spirit to convict with the testimony of scripture. We will say that the arguments put forth by well-known pastors and television evangelists include the notion that our laws already incorporate the tenets of the Ten Commandments. Murder, theft, and perjury, for example, each have explicit references in the Decalogue. The claim is made that the government would be justified in dealing with the remaining elements of moral depravity with a mandate designed to get people into church on Sunday. I wonder, where in the Constitution did the founders write that we must all worship the same God? Although that is what God asked of us, he never said that men must enforce the concept!

> *The churches will see our plight as the result of waning spirituality and unite to urge the government to intervene under the guise of the greater good.*

Functioning Sunday laws already exist in places such as North Dakota, where they proclaim a "day of rest" allegedly to "protect" society from an over indulgence in capitalism. One must ask: if such a law was strictly secular in nature, as its proponents argue, why was the day of rest selected on the same day in which most people choose to worship God? Why did they not choose Monday or Friday and give everyone a three-day weekend? Whether or not the government comes to acknowledge this issue, we must be aware of the religious roots of first day observance. Abstinence from work for one day out of seven has an inherent biblical foundation. But forcing people to stand down from their labors, no matter the motivation or the source of such a decree, is fundamentally contrary to the nature of God's law.

The Bible tells us that those who refuse to accept state dictates because they force the transgression of divine law become the targets of persecution. The instigators of this apostasy will view resistance as an impediment to righting the planet's ills and even the cause of them. Underlying these overt rationales for heinous actions is the most insidious motivation of them all and the single greatest cause of suffering the world has ever known.

"… yea, the time cometh, that whosoever killeth you will think that he doeth God service" (John 16:2).

Throughout history, no other mindset is more responsible for the death of the innocent than misguided religious zealotry. We see it on the news every day. What the Bible refers to in the not-too-distant future is a veritable replay of the inquisition. The Bible says it will happen.

"For nation shall rise against nation, and kingdom against kingdom: and there shall be famines, and pestilences, and earthquakes, in divers places. All these are the beginning of sorrows. Then shall they deliver you up to be afflicted, and shall kill you: and ye shall be hated of all nations for my name's sake" (Matt. 24:7–9).

The apostles were the first to experience this prediction. Brought before tribunals and thrown into prisons, all but one lost his life. This did not conclude prophecy though. John penned Revelation more than twenty years after the last days of Jerusalem. The plight of the holy city and its citizens set the historical precedent for the end of the world. However, John's visions carried him through the history of centuries yet to come. He saw images of the horrific events to occur throughout the Dark Ages, the Protestant reformation, and the French Revolution. He ultimately saw how the persecuting power of papal Rome, temporarily wounded and unable to oppress, would eventually return to power and resume its effort to dominate the religious world. If you believe this scenario is implausible, we will shortly provide the proof that it has already begun.

Chapter 14
The Sabbath–
It's About Worship

*And Elijah came unto all the people, and said, How long halt ye between
two opinions? if the LORD be God, follow him: but if Baal, then follow him.
And the people answered him not a word.*
1 Kings 18:21

Without deviating into a political discussion, the description of the United States in prophecy indicates a foundation of lamb-like benevolence with a tendency to speak like a dragon. In other words, the country transitions to a state of tyranny. Many people see this occurring even now. We seem far from any attempts to implement spiritual solutions to our problems, but the times change quickly and prophecy says the scenario is inevitable.

In colonial times, church attendance was often mandatory. Some states even wrote capital punishment into their laws for repeat offenders. Later, the Blue Laws presented a softer, more subtle imposition on the freedom to worship according to one's conscience. Inevitably even those measures led to persecution, vigilantism, and neighbors ratting out neighbors. There is only one spiritual institution, common to both Catholicism and Protestantism, which has seen the force of law behind it—first day observance, the Sunday worship.

Without stretching the limits of the imagination, forcing people to comply with doctrine is the most obvious means a theocracy might employ to maintain control under the guise of preventing moral decay. Mandatory rest and worship attendance is the only measure the majority of churches have ever agreed to. That eventuality is the reason Revelation reiterates the importance of the Sabbath. As it was in the past, it is unavoidable that such efforts become futile exercises in disciplinary action instead of spiritual growth.

In the future, as it was in 1888, the stated intent of the measure will be to prevent the ruin of society on every conceivable front—social, economic, financial, and even environmental. According to scripture the planet is heading towards its demise. It is not difficult to imagine the formation of an inappropriate relationship between church and state to fashion the necessary mandate to "protect" the masses. But how do we construe this development, one intended to safeguard the population, as the imposition of false worship?

Today, the vast majority of Christians observe religious activity on the first day, and they use many rationales to justify it. God will respect most any sincere, reverent, and innocent worship. This is why the Bible says God has people everywhere. The problem occurs when it becomes a requirement dictated by men. In such a case, the authenticity of that tribute becomes tainted because it may no longer be a fruit of the Holy Spirit or an expression of free will.

The Sunday church service is a creation of the papal system, and they proudly declare their change of the holy day as a mark of their ecclesiastical authority, "He shall … think to change times and laws" (Dan. 7:25). The Church also admits first-day worship has no biblical basis. However, as we stated, Catholicism does not derive most of its dogma from scripture, but from tradition. Protestants, on the other hand, founded on the concept of *Sola Scriptura*, aim to rely exclusively on the Bible for doctrine. But most don't realize that by keeping the first day instead of the biblical Sabbath, they are paying homage to the Papacy.

Many Protestants reason that first-day worship commemorates the resurrection of Christ. Recognition of this seminal event is an integral part of any weekly church service and even our daily prayers. However, there is no biblical requirement to honor the resurrection on a specific day or any day for that matter, including Easter. The Sabbath is different. God hallowed and sanctified the seventh-day to memorialize His act of Creation and establish His dominion as Lord over the entire universe (see Gen. 2:2, 3). Moreover, just as God chose the means for Adam and Eve to show their allegiance, the Lord set the fourth commandment in the midst of the Decalogue for that same purpose. It is not up to us to choose the day. How could it be? Only the One who rules can authorize the means to pay homage, and God never set apart the first-day in tribute to anything.

For those who believe the Sabbath was a ceremonial ordinance that God only required the Jews to observe, we must point out that there were no Jews at Creation. English Bibles often epitomize the term "lost in translation." The Hebrew word from which translators took "rested" in Genesis 2:2 and 3 is *shabath*. This shows that God literally "sabbathed" on the seventh-day. When Moses received the Ten Commandments at Sinai, the fourth commandment began with the word "Remember." One cannot be expected to remember something if it did not already exist. That bears repeating. One cannot "remember" something if it did not already exist. Prior to its inscription on stone tablets, the knowledge of the Sabbath and the commandments in general passed from generation to generation by word of mouth. Men are notoriously "forgetful" and on several occasions, before the Jews ever reached Mt. Sinai, they received cautions from the Lord for the proper observance of His holy day.

Many modern churches pigeonhole certain verses and then form a set of beliefs from an incomplete understanding. Texts such as Colossians 2:16, if studied without any comparison to the Old Testament, are easily misconstrued. The ordinances, which Jesus nailed to the cross, are not the Ten Commandments. What Paul mentions here were special days, also called sabbaths (see Lev. 16 and 23), which were part of the feasts and other ritual celebrations pointing forward to the ministry of Christ. These became obsolete because the priesthood of Jesus fulfills them all. Read Colossians 2 in its greater context.

"Blotting out the handwriting of ordinances that was against us, which was contrary to us, and took it out of the way, nailing it to his cross; And having spoiled principalities and powers, he made a shew of them openly, triumphing over them in it. Let no man therefore judge you in meat, or in drink, or in respect of an holyday, or of the new moon, or of the sabbath days:

Which are a shadow of things to come; but the body is of Christ" (Col. 2:14–17).

The fourth commandment is not of the celebratory or symbolic nature, which Paul refers to in the book of Colossians. Unfortunately, some highly prominent Christian leaders teach it that way. Consider what Paul said about those ordinances. "Blotting out the handwriting of ordinances that was against us, which was contrary to us, and took it out of the way … " The handwriting of ordinances is the Law of Moses, not the Ten Commandments, which God personally engraved on stone to demonstrate His eternal and unchanging character, and thus His Law.

"And it came to pass, when Moses had made an end of writing the words of this law in a book, until they were finished, That Moses commanded the Levites, which bare the ark of the covenant of the LORD, saying, Take this book of the law, and put it in the side of the ark of the covenant of the LORD your God, that it may be there for a witness against thee" (Deut. 31:24–26).

Man was never meant to feel that the Commandments were contrary to us. "But his delight is in the law of the LORD; and in his law doth he meditate day and night" (Ps. 1:2). "Great peace have they which love thy law: and nothing shall offend them" (Ps. 119:165). The written law on the other hand levied a heavy burden on the Jews. The new covenant should have come as a profound blessing to anyone who labored under those constraints. In spite of Paul's explanation, many Jews would not accept the new reality and continued to observe many of the old ordinances while insisting that new converts do the same. Many Christians today take Paul's teaching to the opposite end of the interpretation and believe we are bound by no laws at all! Paul dealt with that issue too.

"Do we then make void the law through faith? God forbid: yea, we establish the law" (Rom. 3:31).

Another common rationale for brushing aside the Sabbath truth is the calendar. Ironically, the same people who enthusiastically hold up Sunday as the resurrection day and Easter cannot seem to agree that the Sabbath occurs on the seventh day, which is Saturday. This is in spite of the fact that the Jews still observe the day after thousands of years. Also notable is the fact that in over 100 languages (English being one of the few exceptions) the word for the seventh-day is a derivation of the Hebrew word, *Shabbath*.

The Bible provides crystal clear proof that the Sabbath is the day that preceded the resurrection. Those who tended to the body of Christ rested on the Sabbath, according to the commandment. Jesus also rested. On the third day, which was the first day of the week, Christ rose.

"This man went unto Pilate, and begged the body of Jesus. And he took it down, and wrapped it in linen, and laid it in a sepulchre that was hewn in stone, wherein never man before was laid. And that day was the preparation, and the sabbath drew on. And the women also, which came with him from Galilee, followed after, and beheld the sepulchre, and how his body was laid. And they returned, and prepared spices and ointments; and rested the sabbath day according to the commandment"

(Luke 23:52–56).

"Now upon the first day of the week, very early in the morning, they came unto the sepulchre, bringing the spices which they had prepared, and certain others with them.

And they found the stone rolled away from the sepulchre. And they entered in, and found not the body of the Lord Jesus" (Luke 24:1–3).

There was never a biblical inference that Christ did away with the fourth or any other commandment. Loving God supremely and one's neighbor as himself are enshrined in every facet of the Decalogue. With respect to the Sabbath itself, Jesus said this:

"And he said unto them, The sabbath was made for man, and not man for the sabbath:

Therefore the Son of man is Lord also of the sabbath" (Mark 2:27, 28).

In regard to keeping the Sabbath in years to come, the Lord conveyed this clear admonition in Matthew 24: "When ye therefore shall see the abomination of desolation, spoken of by Daniel the prophet, stand in the holy place, (whoso readeth, let him understand:) Then let them which be in Judaea flee into the mountains" (Matt. 24:15, 16).

> *"Do we then make void the law through faith? God forbid: yea, we establish the law" (Rom. 3:31).*

"But pray ye that your flight be not in the winter, neither on the sabbath day: For then shall be great tribulation, such as was not since the beginning of the world to this time, no, nor ever shall be" (Matt. 24:20, 21).

Jesus makes no concessions about the importance of the Sabbath in the future, even in the midst of persecution or strife. Does this mean we have to drive to church in the middle of a typhoon or a hailstorm? Obviously no, the claims made by some that Sabbath observance is a Draconian holdover from the Old Testament are without merit. It is a blessing to commune with the Lord in whatever or wherever one's circumstances happen to put them. We observe the Sabbath out of love for God, not a sense of obligation. Fellowship on the day is desirable and beneficial, but it does not require foolish risks.

In AD 364, the Council of Laodicea decreed Sunday observance for Christians. The alleged goal of Canon 29 was to prevent the "judaization" of the Catholic religion. Interestingly, this was because Jews refrained from work on the Sabbath. This decree proves that Christians were Sabbath-keeping people well into the fourth century and that Sunday is not the Sabbath. The canon denounced those who did not comply with the church dictate. As a result, first day observance fell under the purview of the church and her concepts of religious service instead of scripture's.

During the reformation, new churches sprang from the reinvigorated precept of righteousness by faith. For centuries, Romanism insisted that works of penance and homage to the Holy See were requisites for salvation. Martin Luther and many other brave souls opened the scriptures to many for the first time, and the chains of spiritual oppression finally came off as people realized the nature of their captivity. However, Protestants had lost sight of the Sabbath. Though many acknowledged that the Bible said nothing about Sunday sacredness, the seventh-day remained stigmatized by the perception of its "Jewish" origin. Today, the knowledge of the Sabbath still suffers under that same error.

One of the most common and perhaps most insurmountable excuses people use to maintain their traditions is the belief that the day simply does not matter. While none of the reasons used to honor the "Lord's Day" bear up under Bible scrutiny, this one is the most illogical. God never gave man the right to determine what precepts comprised the Ten Commandments or the manner in which He expected us to honor them. Why would the Sabbath be any different? The Lord numbered the days in each stage of creation, and on the final day, the seventh day, He rested. It was that specific day that He hallowed and set apart for worship. How can we arbitrarily decide that the third or the fifth day are just as holy?

As it is with any commandment, the proper observance of the Sabbath requires a special commitment and a change of lifestyle that many are unwilling to make. In general, most churches regard deference to "Old Testament teachings" as obsolete and obedience thereof as an act of fruitless legalism.

The Sabbath, though, is no more a relic of the Jewish faith than the command not to kill or steal. Were only Jews governed by those commandments? Sadly, many people view the law as constraining, limiting, and controlling. That is not how God wants us to understand His government. Jesus tells us that our love for Him is the rationale for keeping His commandments. The character in harmony with the divine will does not feel a burden in obedience. God sanctified and established the Sabbath for all men to remember and keep holy. We do not follow His commandments because we think it will save us, which is the mindset of legalism. The quality of our obedience can never do that, but a sincere effort is the fruit of the Holy Spirit, an act of faith, and the proof that we love our Creator, Jesus Christ.

Finally, circling back now to our opening topic for this chapter, the wanton relationship between the great harlot, spiritual Babylon, and the kings of the earth ultimately becomes a coalition of wrath toward commandment-keeping people. That is what Elijah experienced in his conflict with the pagan sorceress, Jezebel. She along with the false prophets of Baal manipulated her weak and pliable husband, King Ahab. That is how John the Baptist, the second Elijah, fell at the command of Herod, urged on by his adulterous wife, Herodius, and her daughter, Salome. Jesus was also a victim of the state manipulated by the church and its false prophets. Ultimately, that is what happened to Christians for twelve centuries in Europe, and it is already happening again to Christians in the last days.

While the means of escape from this system and avoiding the mark of the beast could entail a physical departure from certain places of worship, it more specifically requires us to walk in the manner God has prescribed from the beginning: with a repentant heart and obedient to His commandments. We must realize that our salvation rests on the merits of Christ's righteousness and not our own, but at the same time demonstrate a faith that works by love, and therefore, obedience.

Our refusal to accept a human law in the place of God's does not run counter to the biblical precept to submit ourselves to the authorities God ordains for the purpose of maintaining an orderly society. Enforced worship is not the will of God. Escape may be a term relative to one's geographical circumstances, but not their spirituality. When the choice becomes clear, we must choose one side or the other, worship the image or worship the Creator.

In places where the enforcement of the image is intense and relentless, refusing the mark of the beast may require an overt act of civil disobedience. Submission to an apostate law to avoid consequences may spare one from the wrath of men, but God will notice the rejection of His will.

Persecution is a foregone conclusion, but it does not mean one has to go looking for it. Abel was certainly not. Jesus evaded His enemies on several occasions, and Elijah ran for his life to escape the wrath of Jezebel. Christ told His followers in Jerusalem to flee the city when they saw the sign spoken of by Daniel the prophet.

"When ye therefore shall see the abomination of desolation, spoken of by Daniel the prophet, stand in the holy place, (whoso readeth, let him understand:) Then let them which be in Judaea flee into the mountains" (Matt. 24:15, 16).

"But when ye shall see the abomination of desolation, spoken of by Daniel the prophet, standing where it ought not, (let him that readeth understand,) then let them that be in Judaea flee to the mountains" (Mark 13:14).

"And when ye shall see Jerusalem compassed with armies, then know that the desolation thereof is nigh. Then let them which are in Judaea flee to the mountains; and let them which are in the midst of it depart out; and let not them that are in the countries enter thereinto" (Luke 21:20, 21).

Each of these passages helps us piece together the meaning of the cryptic reference to Daniel 9:27. In Matthew, the text refers to an abomination standing in the Holy Place. This is a reference to the temple. In our case this refers to the church. In the book of Mark, the Bible says the outrage will stand where it ought not. Lastly, Luke says the desolation coincides with the arrival of an army.

In AD 70, Roman legions surrounded Jerusalem bearing symbols of paganism on their standards, most notably those of sun worship. This was the sign of the temple's impending desolation: a pagan emblem planted in the midst of the Holy City. Every Christian of that time escaped the city unharmed. However, thousands of Jews died in the assault, and the temple saw not one stone left upon another, just as Christ predicted.

Today, final fulfillment of that prophecy is unfolding. There are forces massing that will ultimately confront the spiritual city of God's true people, not in the Middle East, but in every corner of the globe. They will erect an abomination similar to the pagan symbols of ancient Rome, and it will stand in the temple, the church of God. In the Most Holy Place of the sanctuary is the repository of God's Holy law, the ark of the covenant. When men erect a law that tramples upon the Ten Commandments, the abomination of desolation is standing in the church and in the hearts and minds of men.

Chapter 15
Ritual and Ruin

It is the spirit that quickeneth; the flesh profiteth nothing: the words that I speak unto you, they are spirit, and they are life.
John 6:63

The rationale behind most smooth doctrines is the appeasement of certain wants or fears. Ironically, if one understands the truth, there should be no cause for grief. Unfortunately, the basis of most misgivings about the gospel are not what people fail to understand, but rather, what they refuse to accept. We do bear the responsibility for our eternal destiny. Jesus shows us the narrow way and gives is strength for the journey, but the path to salvation is not an escalator to heaven. It requires patience, perseverance, and yes, a struggle with oneself.

The opposite of doing nothing in our Christian experience is trying to do that which is unnecessary or even counterproductive. With respect to the former, it is impossible for our works to save us. Our righteousness is but filthy rags (see Isa. 64:6). But many have succumbed to the notion that they must earn their salvation by acts of penance and scripted prayer. This leads to a legalistic Christian experience, one performed out of obligation instead of love. Such a religion engenders no true freedom in Christ. It only gives one a life of drudgery. When taught about this danger, many go to the other extreme because they believe that works of any kind are pointless. Nevertheless ...

"Yea, a man may say, Thou hast faith, and I have works: shew me thy faith without thy works, and I will shew thee my faith by my works" (James 2:18).

One means of comfort we should draw from is the truth that our hope lies in Christ's righteousness, not our own. Trusting in His ability to overcome is the key to our salvation. However, we cannot let that fact allow us to think our works are pointless. The effort we put forth to win the battle over sin demonstrates our faith, love, and commitment to God.

However, there are things, which some believers do, that fall outside of the Holy Spirit's teaching. The effort to earn salvation through works, which truly are unnecessary and pointless, leads people into an equally false sense of security, or worse, a self-righteous Christian experience.

Many of the Jews would not abandon the ceremonial ordinance after the establishment of the new covenant. They never grasped the symbolism that should have pointed them to the true Lamb of God.

A sacrament is among many Christians that supposedly does more than point to Christ; it professes the power to transform one into His likeness. Ironically, the Lord did establish an ordinance of worship, which forms the basis of this ritual. An enormous number of professed believers have succumbed to the notion that one particular version of this practice harbors the mystical ability to alter one's character from within. We will examine that concept in some detail.

We said at the outset of this writing that a detailed examination of spiritual Babylon's doctrines was impractical. We must make an exception in this particular case for reasons that will become even more apparent in the coming pages. But before we embark on the Bible study of this subject, I must emphasize that this expose is not a criticism of those who participate in the practice. It is a plea to understand its fallacy. A person's intentions may be sincere, but that does not mean they are not sincerely deceived.

"And as they were eating, Jesus took bread, and blessed it, and brake it, and gave it to the disciples, and said, Take, eat; this is my body. And he took the cup, and gave thanks, and gave it to them, saying, Drink ye all of it; For this is my blood of the new testament, which is shed for many for the remission of sins" (Matt. 26:26–28).

"And he took bread, and gave thanks, and brake it, and gave unto them, saying, This is my body which is given for you: this do in remembrance of me. Likewise also the cup after supper, saying, This cup is the new testament in my blood, which is shed for you" (Luke 22:19, 20).

During His Last Supper, Christ confirmed a new ceremony to His followers. We know it commonly as Communion. Many Christian denominations partake of this ritual in some manner. Some conduct the ritual weekly while others do so less often. The Bible makes no stipulation as to the frequency, only its purpose, remembrance. The communion service is a ritual that helps us reflect on the importance of Christ's sacrifice. It is not an occasion to take casually or with an air of frivolity.

"For as often as ye eat this bread, and drink this cup, ye do shew the Lord's death till he come. Wherefore whosoever shall eat this bread, and drink this cup of the Lord, unworthily, shall be guilty of the body and blood of the Lord. But let a man examine himself, and so let him eat of that bread, and drink of that cup. For he that eateth and drinketh unworthily, eateth and drinketh damnation to himself, not discerning the Lord's body" (1 Cor. 11:26–29).

The significance of Christ's death cannot be understated. The King and Creator of the universe lowered himself to the level of sinful human beings to save us from the scourge of sin. It staggers the mind to consider how and why a God that big would do that. Notwithstanding His power to accomplish anything, including the greatest miracle of all in our conversion, there are no biblical texts that say partaking of bread and wine in this tradition was anything more than a commemorative service.

This is not a harmless aberration from the biblical teaching. The dogma behind this concept has millions convinced that their salvation depends on partaking of the ritual. Moreover, the Church, which promotes this teaching, insists that the practice is a requisite for unity within the body of Christ, as a whole. This means all churches. You may read their philosophy for yourselves:

> Since the holy Eucharist is "the wonderful sacrament … by which the unity of the Church

is both signified and brought about," it is very important to see that it is celebrated well so that the faithful can participate in it, because "by offering the Immaculate Victim not only through the hands of the priest but also with him, they should learn to offer themselves too. Through Christ the Mediator they should be drawn day by day into ever closer union with God and with each other, so that finally God may be all in all."[1]

We speak of the Eucharist, the communion service as practiced by the Catholic Church. Why is this ritual a problem? Why do we single out this church's doctrines for criticism once again? It is unfortunate that our discussion appears to harp on many of the mechanisms of Romanism. But we do so to defend the spiritual foundations of the gospel and also demonstrate a rationale behind the practice of this ritual that could very well facilitate the acceptance of a Sunday worship mandate.

Catholicism teaches that partaking of sacramental bread and ceremonial wine allows everyone to eat and drink their way to the similitude of Christ. The doctrine submits that through a miracle known as transubstantiation, allegedly performed each time a priest conducts the ceremony, Christ's flesh and blood, or at least its essence, literally manifests in the bread and wine. According to the Church, by consuming the "body of Christ," participants in the Eucharist assimilate the divine nature. Moreover, Catholicism asserts that because Jesus shed His blood for the remission of sins, the transubstantiated wine cleanses the consumer from sins of their past and preserves them from sins in the future. There is a Bible text from which the church derived this concept.

"Then Jesus said unto them, Verily, verily, I say unto you, Except ye eat the flesh of the Son of man, and drink his blood, ye have no life in you. Whoso eateth my flesh, and drinketh my blood, hath eternal life; and I will raise him up at the last day" (John 6:53, 54).

We spoke previously about the dangers of building a theology around a single passage of scripture. An isolated interpretation of these two texts is the foundation of such an error. Can one imagine the type of churches that might exist within Christianity if these were the only two texts one ever studied? Christ knew the concept in verse 53 was difficult to comprehend. He knew some men would take His words literally. Many did so the moment he spoke them! That is why this "hard saying" turned some would-be disciples away (see John 6:60, 66). Yet, Christ goes on to explain ...

"It is the spirit that quickeneth; the flesh profiteth nothing: the words that I speak unto you, they are spirit, and they are life" (John 6:63).

Why did Jesus appear to confuse the matter in the first place? Why did he refer to himself in the bizarre context of nutritional consumption? He was using a metaphor for what it means to make the Word a part of us. We eat and drink to grow and stay healthy. The same concept applies to growth in spirit. What Christ refers to is not His literal flesh or any semblance of it. He is the Word made flesh, He is the manna sent from heaven, and He is the Bread of Life, not physically but spiritually. The Word is

---

1   "Directory for the Application of Principles and Norms on Ecumenism," Vatican, http://www.vatican.va/roman_curia/pontifical_councils/chrstuni/general-docs/rc_pc_chrstuni_doc_19930325_directory_en.html#top (accessed February 19, 2013).

the sustenance of a life that gains its strength and nourishment from God.

One might argue that the Eucharistic celebration symbolizes the same thing. That might seem reasonable to those unfamiliar with the Catholic dogma behind it. But the doctrine of transubstantiation fashions its rationale from the notion that a priest conjures the body of Christ in a wafer and the reconstituted blood of Jesus in the form of wine. It is believed that these become a literal part of the person who consumes them. In this way, the church teaches that their version of the ritual is more than symbolic; it alleges a literal power to convert! Jesus never said that was the purpose for the ceremony, and His words in John 6:63 confirm it.

> *"It is the spirit that quickeneth; the flesh profiteth nothing: the words that I speak unto you, they are spirit, and they are life" (John 6:63).*

The sacrament of the Eucharist is a form of mysticism. No matter how one tries to infuse it with spirituality, it does not have the power to convert any one. It is only by the grace of God that Jesus becomes a "part" of us. It is the Word, which gives us life; it is the Spirit, which quickens us. Jesus is the Word and the only way God's Spirit will make the Word part of us is when we hear the Word, obey the Word, share the Word, and live the Word!

Friends, there are no rituals that will cause a person to grow to Christian maturity. God will perform in us the miracle of conversion only by our faithful and loving submission to the pleadings of the Holy Spirit. The communion service is a memorial to Christ, which calls to mind what He did for us and what it means to partake of Him. It helps us to appreciate His incredible sacrifice and encourages us to consecrate our lives to Him in humble service. Jesus said, "… This do in remembrance of me" (Luke 22:19).

Nevertheless, communion is a sacred ceremony. Much like baptism, engaging in the ritual is only suitable for people who fully understand its meaning and appreciate its value. To cherish any known sin while one participates in a communion is a grievous mistake. It is essential that we discern the spiritual, not literal, meaning for the term, "Body of Christ."

Within the context of the statement by the Pontifical Council for Promoting Christian Unity, one might presume the unity brought about by the "wonderful sacrament" refers only to the body of faithful Catholics. However, we read this from the same narrative:

> Since the celebration of the Eucharist on the Lord's Day is the foundation and centre of the whole liturgical year, Catholics—but those of Eastern Churches according to their own Law—are obliged to attend Mass on that day and on days of precept. It is not advisable therefore to organize ecumenical services on Sundays, and it must be remembered that even when Catholics participate in ecumenical services or in services of other Churches and ecclesial Communities, the obligation of participating at Mass on these days remains.[2]

The gravity of these statements shall become clearer in the coming pages. Notice the obligatory

---

2   Ibid.

nature of Sunday Mass in the celebration of the Eucharist. This reflects the character of the system. Worship, according to their traditions, is not optional. It is only by the conspicuous lack of state support that the church cannot enforce their will on its members. Little do most know that within the back halls and conference rooms of the religious world, there is a growing movement to rectify this problem.

Chapter 16
Ecumenism– The Unity Façade

Shall the throne of iniquity have fellowship with thee, which frameth mischief by a law?
Psalm 94:20

Except the LORD build the house, they labour in vain that build it.
Psalm 127:1

Throughout Christendom and the greater world community, finding solutions to the burgeoning levels of poverty, hunger, disease, crime, religious extremism, and environmental concerns are at the forefront of nearly every debate. In identifying the moral and social issues facing the planet, there is little agreement among churches about the specific measures necessary to deal with them.

Some believe the world will not make significant progress toward global peace and prosperity until the churches speak with a unified voice. Their purpose is to achieve greater influence over civil authority and sway over public policy. Those who believe divine decree sets the standard of unity in this literal context also proclaim it a requisite for the redemption of humankind. To some, the effort to build this interfaith alliance is the foundation of ecumenism.

The vast majority of public pronouncements and social creeds established by organizations within the unification movement largely address international concerns of a political policy nature. Behind the scenes the movement harbors age-old manifestations of the Catholic Church's goal of a universal church, united under the banner of papal primacy.

> The restoration of unity among all Christians is one of the principal concerns of the Second Vatican Council. Christ the Lord founded one Church and one Church only. However, many Christian communions present themselves to men as the true inheritors of Jesus Christ; all indeed profess to be followers of the Lord but differ in mind and go their different ways, as if Christ Himself were divided. Such division openly contradicts the will of Christ, scandalizes the world, and damages the holy cause of preaching the Gospel to every creature.

> But the Lord of Ages wisely and patiently follows out the plan of grace on our behalf, sinners that we are. In recent times more than ever before, He has been rousing divided Christians to remorse over their divisions and to a longing for unity. Everywhere large numbers have felt the impulse of this grace, and among our separated brethren also there increases from day to day the movement, fostered by the grace of the Holy Spirit, for the restoration of unity among all Christians. This movement toward unity is called "ecumenical." Those belong to it who invoke the Triune God and confess Jesus as Lord and Savior, doing this not merely as individuals but also as corporate bodies. For almost everyone regards the body in which he has heard the Gospel as his Church and indeed, God's Church. All however, though in different ways, long for the one visible Church of God, a Church truly universal and set forth into the world that the world may be converted to the Gospel and so be saved, to the glory of God.[1]

Not long ago, I read an essay pertaining to Christian unity in which the writer praised the diversity of doctrines among churches as an asset to the faith. Supposedly, a multifaceted approach to understanding God is a better vehicle than pure gospel teaching. Ironically, the author mitigated the relevance of strict doctrine and declared that anyone who adheres to a dogmatic interpretation of scripture is emulating a philosophy that Jesus hates, Nicolaitanism. Christ detested the deeds of the Nicolaitans because they were a form of heresy not unlike the concept of cheap grace or guaranteed salvation, which is when one may indulge the desires of the flesh with no consequences for the spirit. That is a concept the Bible clearly does not teach.

"So hast thou also them that hold the doctrine of the Nicolaitans, which thing I hate.

Repent; or else I will come unto thee quickly, and will fight against them with the sword of my mouth" (Rev. 2:15, 16).

Steadfast adherence to biblical precepts is anything but heretical. The Bible encourages us to be zealous towards God and good works (see Titus 2:14 and Rev. 3:19). Unfortunately, many Christians believe that such a fervent faith will label them as a fanatic. When the gospel is misapplied or contorted, the label is often justified. It is the fear of being branded negatively that leads many to compromise their beliefs simply to assuage those who would likely ridicule or even persecute them. This attitude drives much of the Evangelical and Protestant world today as denominations seek a greater accord with Rome to foster that image of unity that the world may believe.

The Protestant reformation was a righteous rebellion against blasphemy, doctrinal error, and spiritual oppression by the papal system. Many present-day churches, which commonly preach smooth or questionable ideas, no longer see the relevance of their separation from Rome. Where early Protestant denominations often quarreled amongst themselves over doctrinal differences, many modern churches rarely even teach from scripture. Incredibly, Romanists frequently refer to scripture more often than

---

[1] "Decree on Ecumenism," Vatican, http://www.vatican.va/archive/hist_councils/ii_vatican_council/documents/vat-ii_decree_19641121_unitatis-redintegratio_en.html (accessed February 19, 2013).

their non-Catholic contemporaries do. In this, we find a most insidious deception. Though they once deemed teaching from the Bible an act of heresy, we now find a generous exposition of scriptural texts touting the virtues and the lordship of Jesus Christ. Do not be fooled. We can discern by statements from the Pontifical Council on Promoting Christian Unity and from the Vatican itself that Rome has not reformed its underlying traits. It has not abandoned its cherished dogma. Moreover, Papists assert that only through their traditions are we capable of understanding scripture. Unfortunately, this allows them to interpret it in any manner they deem appropriate, and we hear protesting from fewer and fewer Bible-based churches.

The public face of ecumenism displays a badly needed visage of compassion and concern for the poor and downtrodden. Toward a solution to their plight and numerous other social issues, many spiritual leaders consider their unity movement an effort to achieve better public policy. However, there is strong evidence to show that many who embrace this philosophy also seek to unify the Christian world in its form of worship.

What is the harm? As stated, one motivation behind this effort is to provide for the common good by globalizing the humanitarian efforts of religion. But how will disparate views on doctrine and even God himself be reconciled (or ignored) in the drive to achieve this goal? Somewhere along the way, somebody must compromise his or her beliefs. Here is a document prepared by the Pontifical Council for Promoting Christian Unity that shows how Catholicism views its role:

> Catholics hold the firm conviction that the one Church of Christ subsists in the Catholic Church "which is governed by the successor of Peter and by the Bishops in communion with him". They confess that the entirety of revealed truth, of sacraments, and of ministry that Christ gave for the building up of his Church and the carrying out of its mission is found within the Catholic communion of the Church. Certainly, Catholics know that personally they have not made full use of and do not make full use of the means of grace with which the Church is endowed. For all that, Catholics never lose confidence in the Church. Their faith assures them that it remains "the worthy bride of the Lord, ceaselessly renewing herself through the action of the Holy Spirit until, through the cross, she may attain to that light which knows no setting". Therefore, when Catholics use the words "Churches", "other Churches", "other Churches and ecclesial Communities" etc., to refer to those who are not in full communion with the Catholic Church, this firm conviction and confession of faith must always be kept in mind.[2]
>
> Concern for restoring unity pertains to the whole Church, faithful and clergy alike. It extends to everyone, according to the potential of each, whether it be exercised in daily Christian living or in theological and historical studies". Bearing in mind the nature of

---

2 "Directory for the Application of Principles and Norms on Ecumenism," Vatican, http://www.vatican.va/roman_curia/pontifical_councils/chrstuni/general-docs/rc_pc_chrstuni_doc_19930325_directory_en.html#top (accessed February 19, 2013).

the Catholic Church, Catholics will find, if they follow faithfully the indications of the Second Vatican Council, the means of contributing to the ecumenical formation, both of individuals and of the whole community to which they belong. Thus the unity of all in Christ will be the result of a common growth and maturing. For God's call to interior conversion and renewal in the Church, so fundamental to the quest for unity, excludes no one.[3]

The Roman Church position on unity is not that Catholics, Protestants, Evangelicals, and other religions must hammer out some sort of compromise on doctrines or sacraments; it is that every other ecclesial community must enter into communion with Rome! This has been the fundamental belief and goal of Catholicism since its establishment. To the extent that Rome refers to compromise in their ecumenical discussions, they use it to acknowledge the minor differences they can overlook in the beliefs and sacraments they already have in common with other faiths. They will not abjure the traditions that distinguish their unique theology, and they insist that their "separated brethren" acknowledge the primacy of the pope.

Those in agreement with this concept of Christian unity extrapolate an inference of temporal authority delegated to them from the texts in which Jesus asserts his own all-inclusive dominion. We shall soon see that some religious entities believe this authority parallels the legislative reach of our governments. The truth is that the only power Christ delegated to His followers was the right to teach the gospel.

"And Jesus came and spake unto them, saying, All power is given unto me in heaven and in earth. Go ye therefore, and teach all nations, baptizing them in the name of the Father, and of the Son, and of the Holy Ghost: Teaching them to observe all things whatsoever I have commanded you: and, lo, I am with you always, even unto the end of the world. Amen" (Matt. 28:18–20).

The ecumenical movement believes Christian unity, which is the spiritual harmony of all those who abide in Christ, is achieved by the literal formation of one physical church that shares a common Eucharistic fellowship. This is both nonsense and extremely dangerous! Such a belief obfuscates the foundations of faith prescribed by the new covenant, substituting for the divine work of the Holy Spirit a human construct! No effort to enforce any form of ecclesial practice or to indoctrinate with manmade traditions can replace the spiritual truth found in God's Word! No coerced semblance of piety and religiosity will unify hearts and minds in the love of Christ!

"There is one body, and one Spirit, even as ye are called in one hope of your calling; One Lord, one faith, one baptism, One God and Father of all, who is above all, and through all, and in you all" (Eph. 4:4–6).

"For the perfecting of the saints, for the work of the ministry, for the edifying of the body of Christ: Till we all come in the unity of the faith, and of the knowledge of the Son of God, unto a perfect man, unto the measure of the stature of the fulness of Christ: That we henceforth be no more children,

---

3   Ibid.

tossed to and fro, and carried about with every wind of doctrine, by the sleight of men, and cunning craftiness, whereby they lie in wait to deceive; But speaking the truth in love, may grow up into him in all things, which is the head, even Christ: From whom the whole body fitly joined together and compacted by that which every joint supplieth, according to the effectual working in the measure of every part, maketh increase of the body unto the edifying of itself in love" (Eph. 4:12–16).

"But we all, with open face beholding as in a glass the glory of the Lord, are changed into the same image from glory to glory, even as by the Spirit of the Lord" (2 Cor. 3:18).

The Bible speaks explicitly about unity in Christ. It warns about the craftiness and deceptions of men and the importance of adhering to one and only one biblical doctrine (see Eph. 4:14). Christians achieve spiritual unity as one body when they reflect the image of Jesus in their lives and this can only happen by the grace and power of God, not a form of worship. Every faithful person plays a role in edifying the church and perfecting our characters, and the motivating force behind it all is love and a commitment to sharing the gospel. The fruit of this transformation brings forth an effective global endeavor to promote peace and ease the burden of poverty. We cannot accomplish spiritual growth by any corporate effort to unite on a platform of error!

"Except the LORD build the house, they labour in vain that build it: except the LORD keep the city, the watchman waketh but in vain" (Ps. 127:1).

The Papacy recognizes that the wind of disparate doctrines threatens Christian unity. Unfortunately, it is their doctrines they seek to install in a universal system of worship. As many Evangelical and Protestant churches grow weaker and increasingly ambivalent toward their own beliefs, Romanism is unwavering.

In a speech in Mexico City in 2008, the pope asserted the necessity of a common Eucharist within the global community. Although much of Christendom partakes of a communion service, remember that Protestants have never ascribed to the Romanist interpretation. Nevertheless, Catholicism will never make concessions on its beliefs for this ritual, which comes with certain requirements for participation, namely, attending the Sunday mass.

Did the pope make this statement in a merely evangelical and philosophical context or was there an insinuation that a literal Eucharistic observance is a fundamental requirement for Christian unity? The answer seems rather obvious. Shortly, I will provide more proof of a collaborative effort towards this goal, emanating from a surprising source.

The member churches that embrace ecumenism currently limit themselves to noble gestures of compassion and missionary work. Eventually, deteriorating global conditions will inspire them to reach for more control. This will require many churches to disavow their stance on certain dogmas, what few they have left, and embrace a form of worship that achieves a human standard of unity.

The Ecumenical movement, principally the Catholic faction, will claim that Christ commands unity, which as far as that statement goes, is true. However, unity in the context of sacramental practices finds its substance in human traditions. Please keep in mind, the Catholic version of communion, the Eucharist, is fashioned after their unique set of beliefs and is practiced exclusively during Sunday mass, an entirely manmade institution. None of this is biblical teaching.

"And honour not his father or his mother, he shall be free. Thus have ye made the commandment of God of none effect by your tradition" (Matt. 15:6).

"And he said unto them, Full well ye reject the commandment of God, that ye may keep your own tradition" (Mark 7:9).

"Beware lest any man spoil you through philosophy and vain deceit, after the tradition of men, after the rudiments of the world, and not after Christ" (Col. 2:8).

I promised some additional evidence to support the effort to standardize, enforce, and corrupt Christian worship. The following is an excerpt from a document prepared by an organization called the National Council of Churches of Christ USA, which is devoted to ecumenism. This organization claims a membership of 100,000 local congregations, supporting 45 million people.

> *Christians achieve spiritual unity as one body when they reflect the image of Jesus in their lives and this can only happen by the grace and power of God, not a form of worship.*

> The purpose of the Faith and Order Commission of the National Council of Churches of Christ is "to call the churches to the goal of visible unity in one faith and in one eucharistic fellowship expressed in worship and common life in Christ, and to advance toward that unity that the world may believe.… To advance toward the goal of visible unity the Faith and Order Commission addresses the theological issues which continue to divide the body of Christ. Sometimes those church-dividing theological issues have a long and complex history. Issues such as the meaning of baptism and eucharist, the nature of justification, the nature of the Church, and authority in the Church have divided the churches for centuries and have thus been the subject of many ecumenical discussions and documents.[4]

Truly, if the ecumenical movement sought to present themselves unified before the world solely within the context of a "common life in Christ," there might be little here to quarrel with. However, this organization (and others such as the World Council of Churches) believes that in order for the church to wield a voice of authority strong enough to dictate public policy, a single, visible, Eucharistic fellowship (worship) must be enjoined by all members. For some, this may seem like a logical assertion for any religion that seeks an influential seat at the table of world affairs, but it will never happen within the confines of a strictly evangelistic effort. Someone will have to enforce it. Here is more from the National Council of Churches of Christ document:

> This concern is particularly pressing for the Christian churches, which have presumed to speak with an authoritative voice on issues of both personal morality and public policy. How

---

[4] "The Authority of the Church in the World Faith and Order Commission," National Council of Churches of Christ in the U.S.A., http://www.ncccusa.org/pdfs/newAOC.pdf (accessed February 18, 2013), p. 1.

can the churches teach and bear witness to the gospel authoritatively in a society in which authority itself is suspect and the churches are divided? The Faith and Order Commission offers this paper, on which many churches have collaborated, with the hope of expressing what the churches can say in common on the authority of the Church in the world.[5]

There is considerable disagreement about the nature of authority, especially as exercised by human beings. Authority is multifaceted: it may be personal and charismatic, corporate and institutional, legal or extra-legal, supported by the power to enforce obedience, or not so supported. This alone contributes to widespread disagreement and confusion as to the definition, nature, and limits of authority.[6]

In North America, Christians expressed the impetus to transform the world in unique ways. When attempts to challenge the dominant social and political order in Europe failed, some communities perceived the region as a gift from God for the purpose of establishing a new uncorrupted society—a city set on a hill. As this original impetus faded, revival movements emphasizing individual redemption, and voluntary social activism sparked the formation of new denominations and the modern missionary movement. These developments brought a renewed interest in the world as a place of proclamation and service but also made the concept of Church authority increasingly problematic in the face of an unprecedented proliferation of new denominations that sometimes competed for congregants within the same geographic region.

Furthermore, the tendency to use church and world as distinct categories was underlined in the United States by the no establishment clause in the Bill of Rights. Early proponents sought to avoid a repetition of Europe's wars of religion and declared enforced uniformity of religion anti-Christian. While some advocates viewed such separation as a means of protecting the church from the influence of secular government, others viewed it as a means of preventing churches from interfering with affairs of state. The combined effect of diversity among United States churches and the idea of separation was that United States churches sought to influence the social and political world primarily through persuasion rather than any form of direct governmental control.[7]

It has become more and more clear in our study of the authority of the Church in the world that the churches need to achieve the "goal of visible unity in one faith and in one Eucharistic fellowship expressed in worship and in common life in Christ, and to advance toward that unity that the world may believe."[8]

Notice the portion of the document that details the impediments to ecumenical goals. The paragraph states that there are disputes as to the nature of authority. Notable here is the debate over the "power

---

5 Ibid., p. 2.
6 Ibid., p. 8.
7 Ibid., p. 21.
8 Ibid., p. 27.

to enforce obedience." In a small but staggering phrase we find that for disagreement to exist there must be factions that believe enforced obedience is necessary! We must ask the question, obedience to what, traffic laws? Ineffective as they may be, secular government already prescribes punitive measures for everything from jaywalking to murder. Many of the social foibles iterated in the latter six commandments of God, those that govern human interaction, the criminal and civil laws of the state already regulate. Obviously, no earthly authority can police the mind. This leaves only one area of enforcement unaccounted for among the myriad of human ordinances that might concern the churches—the worship of God.

Moreover, in this brief but eye-opening portion of the NCCCUSA dissertation, the organization subtly laments the disestablishment of the church in the original foundation of the United States. The document states that "early" proponents of this form of governance believed that a forced uniformity of the church was anti-Christian. Are they suggesting this belief no longer exists? Do you understand this mindset? They also denounce the formation of individual denominations as a detriment to the authority of the church and characterize our country's segregated civil and religious structure as a "tendency." Clearly, this organization believes the United States does not function as they want it to. We find that the disestablishment of church from the state is a concept espoused by Christ himself.

"And Jesus answering said unto them, Render to Caesar the things that are Caesar's, and to God the things that are God's. And they marvelled at him" (Mark 12:17).

They still marvel. The authors of the NCCCUSA manifesto do not comprehend, or worse, reject the reasoning of Jesus and our founding fathers. Disestablishment was not a strategy to protect the church from the state or shield the government from the church. The founders intended separation to protect the people from collaboration between the two! Though this does not mean our leaders must separate their decisions from a Godly conscience or that religious beliefs play no role in the laws we make, the framers of the Constitution established a boundary between church and state to prevent the U.S. from functioning as a theocracy, which squashes the rights of individuals. Our founders remembered the history of Europe. They knew about the repression that inevitably follows the collusion of organized religion and government. They wrote the Bill of Rights in such a manner as to prevent that tragedy from ever happening again. Sadly, the ecumenical movement disparages both the teachings of Jesus and the wisdom of the great men who sought to remove the specter of despotism from the American way of life. The tyranny engendered by such an illicit affair is once again on the rise.

The description of the United States in prophecy drew a contrast between the "two horns like a lamb" and the speech of the dragon. The two concepts are a contradiction demonstrated in the history of this nation. Does the majority of the American public now see the first amendment differently than the founders? Is there widespread clamor to unify church and state beyond the moral outlook that drives our legislation? Indeed, there is in some quarters.

The paper suggests in paragraph 54 that there is an inherent inadequacy in using persuasion to influence public policy. It infers that government control (operating under the auspices of religious leadership) is the preferred solution. The document goes on to lament the apparent inability of the church to combat the influence of "competing authorities" such as secular science and bizarre philosophical ideas. While this organization is correct that these entities have gained a substantial foothold in the realm of public policy and even in the conduct of our legal system, the problem lays in what the National Council of Churches proposes to do about this "loss of authority."

Clearly, this organization imputes obsolescence to the biblical model for evangelism in order to cope with the issues of modern society. My friends, I am not suggesting that gentle persuasion, even when performed in the best Christian sense, will solve all the world's problems. This is not because the gospel lacks any provision for dealing with them; it is simply because human beings will not universally accept the truth, and no one can force them to! Jesus Christ is the best evangelist the world has ever seen, yet we saw how the world received His message. In spite of the fact that Christ knew people would ridicule and scoff at the gospel and in spite of the fact that He knew His gospel was a matter of life and death, the Lord never once suggested any means of convincing the unlearned and the disobedient that went beyond passionate persuasion! Free will is the basis of love. Even God cannot take that from men.

Government programs cannot deal with moral issues because of their inability to change the hearts and minds of citizens. However, as ineffective as secular wisdom is in such matters, we have seen throughout history that the church, when it employs the world's tactics to control society, reaps results that are even more disastrous. Ecclesiastical authority, whether under the Pharisees, the papal system of the middle Ages, or Protestantism during the nineteenth century inevitably leads to civil oppression and tyranny. Such a system must overthrow the God-given right of free choice in order to prosper.

Nevertheless, those obsessed with control have no interest in the lessons of history. In all facets of life, society is sliding into perilous times. We can infer by the assertions of ecumenical agencies that there will come a time when the ultimate manifestation of organized religion, a universal church, will once more leverage the strong arm of the state to enforce its version of religiosity and obedience upon the people. Undoubtedly, there will be those among our political leadership who believe that the enforcement of worship is for the good of society.

Though many non-religious people as well as many understanding Christians would obviously quarrel with the concept of legislated religion, why would such an approach not be an effective means of dealing with societal ills? Might not some people actually find God in this "solution?" Compelling someone to participate in a standardized fellowship neither defines, nor establishes Christian unity. No one finds God by force. Aside from the inevitable persecution that accompanies any form of coerced piety, the Lord desires our expression of love for Him and a character conformed to His image as an act of free will. There is no other way to worship!

Everyone living in Christ allows Christ to live in them (see John 17:21–23). This is what it means to be in harmony or "one" in the faith. Changes that occur by the miracle of conversion yield the fruit of Spirit. We cannot seek to appease the Lord and demonstrate unity to the world through mere outward forms of worship. Nor will rituals, steeped in mysticism and spiritualism, promote a Christ-like change in the human character. Without the desire for true repentance, the Holy Spirit cannot convert us and no amount of time we spend in a church will please God, and if the practice of religion assumes a heretical form, we will fall deeper into the abyss of spiritual darkness.

Chapter 17
Armageddon–
It Happened in the Valley

For we are not contending against flesh and blood, but against the principalities, against the powers, against the world rulers of this present darkness, against the spiritual hosts of wickedness in the heavenly places.
Ephesians 6:12, RSV

Legislated worship will lead to far greater consequences than a society living under the burden of tyranny. Conveyed by the third angel's message, this is the crux of the warning to flee spiritual Babylon.

"And the third angel followed them, saying with a loud voice, If any man worship the beast and his image, and receive his mark in his forehead, or in his hand,

The same shall drink of the wine of the wrath of God, which is poured out without mixture into the cup of his indignation; and he shall be tormented with fire and brimstone in the presence of the holy angels, and in the presence of the Lamb:

And the smoke of their torment ascendeth up for ever and ever: and they have no rest day nor night, who worship the beast and his image, and whosoever receiveth the mark of his name" (Rev. 14:9–11).

The imposition of first-day worship establishes the mark of the beast. When Babylon fulfills this prophecy, the final and most catastrophic events in human history, the seven last plagues, are set in motion. The Bible conveys the unmistakable timing of God's wrath upon the wicked in conjunction with this tragic deviation from God's will.

In addition to the torment decreed for those who worship the beast and his image, the Bible tells us that the saints also must endure for a time. However, it is not the seven plagues they must contend with; it is the wrath of men.

"Here is the patience of the saints: here are they that keep the commandments of God, and the faith of Jesus. And I heard a voice from heaven saying unto me, Write, Blessed are the dead which die in the Lord from henceforth: Yea, saith the Spirit, that they may rest from their labours; and their works do follow them" (Rev. 14:12, 13).

There are two important concepts to glean from these verses. First, true Christians will be on earth during the seven plagues. There is no pre-tribulation rapture. Second, the patience of the saints is incumbent upon their relationship with Christ. They are obedient to the very end and exhibit the same character as the Lord when faced with the prospect of death for the sake of the truth. The passage exhorts the faithful to have patience because it will seem as though God has forsaken them. Even Christ uttered words of dejection on the cross. The anguish Christ felt was a prelude to the second death, a feeling that no believer needs to fear, the awful experience of total separation from God. Jesus did not allow the indescribable loneliness in the departure of the Holy Spirit to compromise His faith. Though He was not to die from his wounds, but from a heart rent by utter dejection, Jesus knew that His mission had been accomplished. As this incredible chapter of Revelation draws to a close, the strife culminates in the event most anticipated by believers: the second coming of Jesus.

"And I looked, and behold a white cloud, and upon the cloud one sat like unto the Son of man, having on his head a golden crown, and in his hand a sharp sickle" (Rev. 14:14).

The appearance of our Lord in the clouds brings tidings of salvation and joy to believers everywhere. But for those who have staked a claim to the kingdom in spiritual Babylon, the image of Jesus will be one of dread. The "sharp sickle" He carries is not an instrument of peace.

"And another angel came out of the temple, crying with a loud voice to him that sat on the cloud, Thrust in thy sickle, and reap: for the time is come for thee to reap; for the harvest of the earth is ripe. And he that sat on the cloud thrust in his sickle on the earth; and the earth was reaped. And another angel came out of the temple which is in heaven, he also having a sharp sickle. And another angel came out from the altar, which had power over fire; and cried with a loud cry to him that had the sharp sickle, saying, Thrust in thy sharp sickle, and gather the clusters of the vine of the earth; for her grapes are fully ripe. And the angel thrust in his sickle into the earth, and gathered the vine of the earth, and cast it into the great winepress of the wrath of God. And the winepress was trodden without the city, and blood came out of the winepress, even unto the horse bridles, by the space of a thousand and six hundred furlongs" (Rev. 14:15–20).

The destruction of the wicked is symbolized by a violent harvest of grapes. There are some who extract geographical references from the "space of a thousand and six hundred furlongs," which supposedly represents the length of Israel. They conclude that this points to the Middle East as the site of fruition for the final battle known as Armageddon. Before we consider that possibility, let us examine Revelation 15. This chapter is a brief interlude where the Bible conveys the joy of those who do not yield to the enforcement of false worship. From the book, *The Great Controversy* by Ellen G. White:

> Upon the crystal sea before the throne, that sea of glass as it were mingled with fire,—so resplendent is it with the glory of God,—are gathered the company that have "gotten the victory over the beast, and over his image, and over his mark, and over the number of his name." [Revelation 15:2.] With the Lamb upon Mount Zion, "having the harps of God," they stand, the hundred and forty and four thousand that were redeemed from

among men; and there is heard, as the sound of many waters, and as the sound of a great thunder, "the voice of harpers harping with their harps." [Revelation 14:1-5; 15:3; 7:14-17] And they sing "a new song" before the throne, a song which no man can learn save the hundred and forty and four thousand. It is the song of Moses and the Lamb,—a song of deliverance. None but the hundred and forty-four thousand can learn that song; for it is the song of their experience,—an experience such as no other company have ever had. "These are they which follow the Lamb whithersoever he goeth." These, having been translated from the earth, from among the living, are counted as "the first-fruits unto God and to the Lamb." "These are they which came out of great tribulation;" [Revelation 14:1-5; 15:3; Revelation 7:14-17.] they have passed through the time of trouble such as never was since there was a nation; they have endured the anguish of the time of Jacob's trouble; they have stood without an intercessor through the final outpouring of God's judgments. But they have been delivered, for they have "washed their robes, and made them white in the blood of the Lamb." "In their mouth was found no guile; for they are without fault" before God. "Therefore are they before the throne of God, and serve him day and night in his temple; and he that sitteth on the throne shall dwell among them." [Revelation 14:1-5; 15:3; Revelation 7:14-17.] They have seen the earth wasted with famine and pestilence, the sun having power to scorch men with great heat, and they themselves have endured suffering, hunger, and thirst. But "they shall hunger no more; neither thirst any more; neither shall the sun light on them, nor any heat; for the Lamb which is in the midst of the throne shall feed them, and shall lead them unto living fountains of waters; and God shall wipe away all tears from their eyes." (*The Great Controversy*, pp. 648, 649)

Moving now to Revelation 16, the Bible expands on the outpouring of God's wrath. The seven last plagues bring a level of despair and ruin to the earth that none of us can comprehend. One after another, each vial of divine retribution gives the apostate no rest and no place to hide. Because they view themselves as victims of obstinacy by those who refuse to worship the beast or his image, they turn their anger toward the remnant of God's faithful. Ultimately, spiritual Babylon stirs the world into a deceived frenzy, and they move to destroy the people who will not yield to her decrees.

"For they are the spirits of devils, working miracles, which go forth unto the kings of the earth and of the whole world, to gather them to the battle of that great day of God Almighty Behold, I come as a thief. Blessed is he that watcheth, and keepeth his garments, lest he walk naked, and they see his shame And he gathered them together into a place called in the Hebrew tongue Armageddon" (Rev. 16:14–16).

A thorough and prayerful study of Revelation 13 through 16 draws out no other conclusion than that Armageddon is the climax of a global campaign to eliminate those who do not submit to the beast or his image. At the height of this conflict will be the glorious second advent of Christ. The Bible conveys not only the blessed hope, but a warning along with it. Do not get caught with your pants down.

"Behold I come as a thief … " Jesus will come when the world least expects it. "Blessed is he that watcheth, and keepeth his garments … " be prepared and keep your faith. Stay sanctified by the Word. "Lest he walk naked, and they see his shame … " those who abandon the vestments of salvation will feel the same loss as the first humans to sin, Adam and Eve. Unfortunately, at this stage, there will be no one to provide a covering for one's nakedness. The blood of the Lamb will no longer atone. The righteousness of Christ will no longer be accessible.

The Bible never mentions nor alludes to geographical Israel. The spiritual application of these texts relies on historical precedent. We can no more assume a temporal meaning from these texts than we could deduce that God turns the wicked into grape juice at the end of Revelation 14. Armageddon is a composite of two words, "har" and "Megiddon." The latter directs us to an ancient battlefield in the Old Testament, but it is not the geography that God wants us to see. The Hebrew prefix, "*har*," translates to mountain, and the Megiddo region is actually a valley. What God wants us to understand is not just the location, but what took place there.

Long ago on a battlefield in Palestine, history portrayed the reality of Armageddon. Through songs of lamentation carried down by generations, the story tells of loss and profound sadness wrought by the death of a great king. Who was this king, and what was it about him that made his loss so grievous? Let us go back to the only verse that refers to the Megiddon valley in a prophetic context. "In that day shall there be a great mourning in Jerusalem, as the mourning of Hadadrimmon in the valley of Megiddon" (Zech. 12:11).

This is where our understanding of Armageddon truly begins. Why were the people mourning? What happened there to bring about such despair? The passage begs for one to dig deeper into its history, impact, and application to the future. Thankfully, we do not have to head to the public library or the internet to obtain this knowledge. The Bible explains it all.

King Josiah was the most beloved by his people and the most devoted to the Lord out of all the Jewish kings in history. Ruling Jerusalem for thirty-one years, from the age of eight, Josiah had brought the Jews back into a right relationship with God. He had thrown down the altars of Baal, purged the land of idolatry, cast out the abominable practices of spiritualism, and restored the proper observance of the Passover. Second Kings and 2 Chronicles record the king's heroic and faithful acts. Here are some of the highlights of his reign.

"And Josiah took away all the abominations out of all the countries that pertained to the children of Israel, and made all that were present in Israel to serve, even to serve the LORD their God. And all his days they departed not from following the LORD, the God of their fathers" (2 Chron. 34:33).

"And the king stood by a pillar, and made a covenant before the Lord, to walk after the Lord, and to keep his commandments and his testimonies and his statutes with all their heart and all their soul, to perform the words of this covenant that were written in this book. And all the people stood to the covenant…. And he put down the idolatrous priests, whom the kings of Judah had ordained to burn incense in the high places in the cities of Judah, and in the places round about Jerusalem; them also that burned incense unto Baal, to the sun, and to the moon, and to the planets, and to all the host of heaven" (2 Kings 23:3, 5).

"And like unto him was there no king before him, that turned to the LORD with all his heart, and with all his soul, and with all his might, according to the law of Moses; neither after him arose there any like him" (2 Kings 23:25).

In spite of Josiah's righteous efforts, his works could not atone for the sins of his predecessor. Jesus said about the scriptures in John 5:39, they are they which testify of me. In all that Christ did while He walked the earth, it would not be enough to pay the price for our transgressions. It would take the Savior's death at the hand of a pagan kingdom to wake the people to the reality of what they had done.

> *In the Valley of Megiddo … the people saw that they had lost the one king who gave them hope and offered them a chance for redemption.*

"Nevertheless Josiah would not turn his face from him, but disguised himself, that he might fight with him, and hearkened not unto the words of Necho from the mouth of God, and came to fight in the valley of Megiddo. And the archers shot at king Josiah; and the king said to his servants, Have me away; for I am sore wounded. His servants therefore took him out of that chariot, and put him in the second chariot that he had; and they brought him to Jerusalem, and he died, and was buried in one of the sepulchres of his fathers. And all Judah and Jerusalem mourned for Josiah. And Jeremiah lamented for Josiah: and all the singing men and the singing women spake of Josiah in their lamentations to this day, and made them an ordinance in Israel: and, behold, they are written in the lamentations (2 Chron. 35:22–25).

Let us circle back now to the book of Zechariah, where the scriptures that helped us understand the loss of a great king at Megiddon also direct our attention to the visage of another king.

"And I will pour upon the house of David, and upon the inhabitants of Jerusalem, the spirit of grace and of supplications: and they shall look upon me whom they have pierced, and they shall mourn for him, as one mourneth for his only son, and shall be in bitterness for him, as one that is in bitterness for his firstborn" (Zech. 12:10).

At Hadadrimmon in the valley of Megiddon, the people mourned the loss of the king who labored to bring the people back to God. Now the Old Testament closes the prophetic loop by pointing us back to the very book where our study of Armageddon began.

"Behold, he cometh with clouds; and every eye shall see him, and they also which pierced him: and all kindreds of the earth shall wail because of him. Even so, Amen" (Rev. 1:7)

The world looks for the climactic event in human history through the prism of global conflict. The imagination of Hollywood diverts the mind to calamity while doctrines of appeasement steer hearts away from the source of persecution, their own faith. Few have their eyes open to the truth. The lamentations and mourning in the Valley of Megiddo were not because Israel was at war with Egypt. It was because on that day, the people saw that they had lost the one king who gave them hope and offered them a chance for redemption. At Armageddon, the mountain of slaughter, everyone will see another King who was slain, Jesus. But the unbelieving world, the persecutors of the faithful, and even

Christians who have not obeyed the gospel will lament the Lord whom they have all pierced. They will wail and mourn because they will finally understand what they have done and what they have lost—the one King who could bring them back to God.

Chapter 18
Every Eye Will See Him— The Second Coming

*I am Alpha and Omega, the beginning and the ending, saith the Lord,
which is, and which was, and which is to come, the Almighty.
Revelation 1:8*

Much of the diversity among Christian beliefs is truly paradoxical. There is only one truth. The vital aspects of the gospel can have but a single interpretation. Jesus could not have died to save man both from their sins and in their sins. A person will not go to heaven when they die and take part in the resurrection when Jesus comes. Attempting to live righteously is not a sin! There are many such contradictions posed by the doctrines of spiritual Babylon. While many Christians harbor an error that may lead to bigger problems, the ultimate deception spoken of by Jesus is not among the commonplace mistakes we find here. In fact, the errors we have studied so far only preface and facilitate the greatest test of faith to confront us all.

The mark of the beast will be difficult enough for many to reconcile. Millions will grapple with abandoning years, even generations of religious tradition, denominational pride, and good old-fashioned fear before they arrive at a decision. Based on the biblical teaching, one might think the plain facts, aided by the Holy Spirit, are enough to sway hearts and minds toward the true worship of God, but the enemy is not going to allow such a clear cut choice without a fight. There is only one event that the Bible speaks about that could fulfill this dire prediction:

"For there shall arise false Christs, and false prophets, and shall shew great signs and wonders; insomuch that, if it were possible, they shall deceive the very elect" (Matt. 24:24).

"And no marvel; for Satan himself is transformed into an angel of light" (2 Cor. 11:14).

The devil's greatest act of delusion will have an influence more powerful than any previous. It will be so convincing as to dupe even the most devout Christian ... that is, if they do not know the truth about the second coming.

"Behold, I have told you before. Wherefore if they shall say unto you, Behold, he is in the desert; go not forth: behold, he is in the secret chambers; believe it not. For as the lightning cometh out of the east, and shineth even unto the west; so shall also the coming of the Son of man be" (Matt. 24:25–27).

In spite of all the prophetic signs—wars and rumors of war, frequent earthquakes, chaotic weather, tidal waves, economic upheaval, and the fulfillment of spiritual revelations in the history of papal Rome and the United States, there are many who cannot accept the possibility that Jesus is coming soon. Understandably, it is a staggering proposition, one that any Christian should anticipate with joy. So why are so many believers ready to delay the second advent when the signs indicate that it could happen sooner rather than later? Atheistic scoffers will say the second coming was imminent in the New Testament too, but some Christians find themselves nodding in agreement! We must answer: the scornfulness of the world is also a sign!

"Knowing this first, that there shall come in the last days scoffers, walking after their own lusts, And saying, Where is the promise of his coming? for since the fathers fell asleep, all things continue as they were from the beginning of the creation" (2 Peter 3:3, 4).

The nearness of the second coming must always be at the forefront of the believer's mind. To those who think they have ample time to evaluate the gospel because there is so much prophecy yet to unfold, we say, how do you know? This is what makes doctrines, which postpone its likelihood, a serious matter. Consider the rationale behind life insurance. Even if one knew the exact the date of their death, they could not wait until that time to purchase a policy. The insurance company might take issue with such a payout. One must plan ahead. Nevertheless, most of us do not know when our time here will expire. It could be forty years or forty minutes. This is a hard reality that most of us do not enjoy pondering, but to postpone our readiness for the inevitable is potentially disastrous. Our eternal destiny does not rely on when Jesus comes back; it relies on our preparation. Have we established an insurance policy with the Lord now? Whether we go to sleep before the event or we are blessed to witness His glorious return, our relationship with Him must already be ratified and have His stamp of approval.

Recall that Jesus spoke about the end times as two distinct events: one for literal Jerusalem and one for the world. When New Testament writers made statements, which included phrases such as, "it is the last time" or "in these last days," they were not wrong. It was the last days for the Jewish city as the spiritual center of God's kingdom for men. The city met its demise in AD 70, forty years after the crucifixion of Christ.

Though it was a small gap, why the delay? Remember the biblical precedent. Many of the Jews rebelled at the edge of Canaan, the Promised Land, when they refused to enter a region they considered impossible to possess because of the imposing stature of the current inhabitants. They were literally giants. Their lack of faith in God's protection and strength, which He had manifested throughout their journey, jeopardized their access to the land flowing with milk and honey, and they spent another forty years wandering in the wilderness. During that time, the factions who angered the Lord were purged from among the innocent.

History repeated itself with the death of Christ. The Jews expected the Messiah to overthrow their Roman oppressors. When it became apparent that the Son of God had not come to battle their enemies for them, the Jews perpetrated their final act of rebellion. Again, they rejected the Lord's plea to enter the Promised Land, this time through the door of salvation, Jesus, who stood right before their eyes.

There are still giants standing in the path to paradise. God still asks us to trust Him as we face the obstacles that lay before us—temptation, persecution, possible loss of family and friends. These are monumental challenges. Will we shrink from them because we rely on the limits of our own strength or will we have the faith of Joshua, Caleb, and Jesus, who trusted in the strong arm of the Father to deliver them the victory? We may not know exactly what our future holds on earth. But by faith, we know what God will do for us when our sojourn here is complete.

> *Our eternal destiny does not rely on when Jesus comes back; it relies on our preparation.*

Paul's statement to the Corinthians regarding Satan's transformation into an "angel of light" was not speculative. Although numerous men in history have come claiming they are the Messiah and their cults have successfully brainwashed members into tragic ends, they pale in comparison to what Satan can and will do. The only deception which can ensnare a majority of Christians around the world is the one that appears to fulfill their greatest hope, the return of Jesus. From the book, *The Great Controversy*, we read an amazing visionary account of this event:

> As the crowning act in the great drama of deception, Satan himself will personate Christ. The church has long professed to look to the Saviour's advent as the consummation of her hopes. Now the great deceiver will make it appear that Christ has come. In different parts of the earth, Satan will manifest himself among men as a majestic being of dazzling brightness, resembling the description of the Son of God given by John in the Revelation. [Revelation 1:13–15.] The glory that surrounds him is unsurpassed by anything that mortal eyes have yet beheld. The shout of triumph rings out upon the air, "Christ has come! Christ has come!" The people prostrate themselves in adoration before him, while he lifts up his hands, and pronounces a blessing upon them, as Christ blessed his disciples when he was upon the earth. His voice is soft and subdued, yet full of melody. In gentle, compassionate tones he presents some of the same gracious, heavenly truths which the Saviour uttered; he heals the diseases of the people, and then, in his assumed character of Christ, he claims to have changed the Sabbath to Sunday, and commands all to hallow the day which he has blessed. He declares that those who persist in keeping holy the seventh day are blaspheming his name by refusing to listen to his angels sent to them with light and truth. This is the strong, almost overmastering delusion. Like the Samaritans who were deceived by Simon Magus, the multitudes, from the least to the greatest, give heed to these sorceries, saying, This is "the great power of God." [Acts 8:10.]" (p. 624)

It may seem that there is little means to overcome such a powerful deception. Indeed, many will fall victim to the charms of this false Christ. How can one who does not know the truth resist the lie? The words of Jesus provide a hedge, a method to determine that this is a great delusion. Ellen White continues:

> But the people of God will not be misled. The teachings of this false Christ are not in accordance with the Scriptures His blessing is pronounced upon the worshipers of the beast and his image,–the very class upon whom the Bible declares that God's unmingled wrath shall be poured out.
>
> And, furthermore, Satan is not permitted to counterfeit the manner of Christ's advent. The Saviour has warned his people against deception upon this point, and has clearly foretold the manner of his second coming. "There shall arise false christs, and false prophets, and shall show great signs and wonders; insomuch that, if it were possible, they shall deceive the very elect. . . . Wherefore if they shall say unto you, Behold, he is in the desert; go not forth: behold, he is in the secret chambers; believe it not. For as the lightning cometh out of the east, and shineth even unto the west; so shall also the coming of the Son of man be." [Matthew 24:24–27, 31; 25:31; Revelation 1:7; 1 Thessalonians 4:16, 17.] This coming, there is no possibility of counterfeiting. It will be universally known–witnessed by the whole world.
>
> Only those who have been diligent students of the Scriptures, and who have received the love of the truth, will be shielded from the powerful delusion that takes the world captive. By the Bible testimony these will detect the deceiver in his disguise. (*The Great Controversy*, pp. 624, 625)

Now that we know what to look for, is this enough to safeguard one from entrapment? It depends on how one conducts their affairs in response to the warnings. Will they order their lives in a manner to withstand the trial? Or will doubt and the distractions of modern life delay their preparation? Ellen White continues:

> To all, the testing time will come. By the sifting of temptation, the genuine Christian will be revealed. Are the people of God now so firmly established upon his Word that they would not yield to the evidence of their senses? Would they, in such a crisis, cling to the Bible, and the Bible only? Satan will, if possible, prevent them from obtaining a preparation to stand in that day. He will so arrange affairs as to hedge up their way, entangle them with earthly treasures, cause them to carry a heavy, wearisome burden, that their hearts may be overcharged with the cares of this life, and the day of trial may come upon them as a thief. (*The Great Controversy*, p. 625)

There will come a time to flee the cities and towns where persecution of the faithful will be the most rampant, but God is calling his people to come out of Babylon right now. Those who do not heed the warning and continue to trust in the arm of flesh for their redemption will one day realize the way of escape too late. But perhaps we have not adequately answered the question in some minds. Where does one go to flee Babylon? If one understands and accepts the warnings revealed in scripture and comprehend the explanations given here, then they know that the manner of escape rests in one's allegiance to God through obedience to His commandments and harboring the faithful testimony of Jesus.

The place of escape is to the heart and mind in Christ. Does this mean one has to join a different church? The power of corporate prayer and the spiritual support offered by fellowship cannot be underestimated. The Bible, indeed, stresses its importance. In the final days and hours before the probation of man closes and the judgment era is complete, many will find themselves as the thief on the cross, genuinely repentant, but thinking they have no place to go. Come to Jesus.

Let not your heart be troubled. If you seek God, He will be with you. He will not look for the label of any particular congregation to determine our worthiness. Many churches teach the character and love that Jesus wants to us have. But there is no guarantee that everyone in any particular church, even the one which espouses this biblical doctrine, will see the glory of salvation. Redemption is not about our church membership. It is about the heart. Every repentant soul who hears the call to worship the Creator and rejects the mark of the beast will enter into the joy of the Lord. The message is not a call to abandon the doctrines that a church has right; it is about hearing the plea to escape the teachings that will lead to death.

"Blessed are they that do his commandments, that they may have right to the tree of life, and may enter in through the gates into the city" (Rev. 22:14).

May the truth find its place in you and the love of God abound in your heart. The grace of our Lord Jesus Christ be with you all. Amen.

We invite you to view the complete
selection of titles we publish at:

www.TEACHServices.com

Scan with your mobile
device to go directly
to our website.

Please write or email us your praises, reactions, or
thoughts about this or any other book we publish at:

P.O. Box 954
Ringgold, GA 30736

info@TEACHServices.com

TEACH Services, Inc., titles may be purchased in bulk for
educational, business, fund-raising, or sales promotional use.
For information, please e-mail:

BulkSales@TEACHServices.com

Finally, if you are interested in seeing
your own book in print, please contact us at

publishing@TEACHServices.com

We would be happy to review your manuscript for free.

www.ingramcontent.com/pod-product-compliance
Lightning Source LLC
Chambersburg PA
CBHW081924170426
43200CB00014B/2823